HANDBOOK TO
THE CHURCH HYMNARY
SUPPLEMENT

HANDBOOK TO
THE CHURCH HYMNARY
SUPPLEMENT

EDITED BY

The Rev. MILLAR PATRICK
D.D.

OXFORD UNIVERSITY PRESS
LONDON : HUMPHREY MILFORD
1935

OXFORD
UNIVERSITY PRESS
AMEN HOUSE, E.C. 4
London Edinburgh Glasgow
New York Toronto Melbourne
Capetown Bombay Calcutta
Madras Shanghai
HUMPHREY MILFORD
PUBLISHER TO THE
UNIVERSITY

PRINTED IN GREAT BRITAIN

CONTENTS

v

PRINCIPAL AUTHORITIES CONSULTED
(Additional)

Nelle, Wilhelm, *Schlüssel zum Evangelischen Gesangbuch für Rheinland und Westfalen* (1924).

Raby, F. J. E., *A History of Christian-Latin Poetry from the beginning to the close of the Middle Ages* (1927).

Jones, J. Edmund, *The Book of Common Praise* (Canada), *Annotated Edition* (1909).

Dearmer, Percy, and Jacob, Archibald, *Songs of Praise Discussed* (1933).

Lightwood, James T., *The Music of the Methodist Hymn Book* (1935).

PREFACE

THE publication of the *Handbook* was hastened in 1927 in order that it might synchronize with the appearance of *The Revised Church Hymnary*. Its value, its sponsors felt, would to some extent depend upon its being available at once upon the publication of the book on which it was a commentary. A price had to be paid, however, for the advantages of this immediacy of issue: there was no opportunity for a final deliberate and comprehensive survey of the material, with a view to eliminating errors and supplying deficiencies.

The *errata*, considering the large amount of historical detail involved, have been found to be extraordinarily few; but it is right that they should be corrected. Omissions have been more numerous, and though none of them is serious, it is desirable that they should be made good. Additional material has been gathering also in the intervening years. It has been thought worth while, therefore, to issue a Supplement to the *Handbook*, presenting all the *corrigenda* and *addenda* that have been found to be required.

It has been deemed opportune, at the same time, to offer annotations, similar to those on the hymn-tunes, on those tunes in *The Scottish Psalter 1929*, *Metrical Version*, which were not included in the *Hymnary*. To have dealt in the same way with the chants in the *Prose Version* would have demanded an amount of research out of all proportion to any value or even interest in the result, and it has not been thought necessary to attempt such a task. Biographical notes, however, on the composers represented in both versions who have not already received attention in the *Handbook*, have been thought likely to prove welcome.

The preparation of all this material fell naturally to the present editor. It was on his initiative that the *Handbook* was undertaken; he was chairman of the group of collaborators who assembled the material; and in the end the editorship itself devolved on him when Dr. Moffatt, called to New York, was obliged to relinquish an uncompleted task.

Preface

Various obligations must gratefully be expressed: to the late James Love's *Scottish Church Music*, the pioneer book of this kind; to the work of the late William Cowan, that admirable scholar, whose invincible modesty and inflexible austerity of style concealed an accomplishment, in the field of the music of psalmody and hymnody, as wide in its range as it was unassailable in its accuracy; to Miss Anne G. Gilchrist, learned alike in folk-song and in the history of church tunes, for a number of interesting identifications of sources and for other invaluable assistance; to Mr. James T. Lightwood, editor of *The Choir* and author of *Hymn Tunes and their Story*, for much friendly suggestion; to Mr. Humphrey Milford, of the Oxford University Press, who, having received willing permission for Canon Dearmer to draw *ad libitum* upon the contents of the *Handbook* for *Songs of Praise Discussed* (1933), has reciprocated the courtesy by allowing the use of such extracts from the latter book as are useful for the present purpose; to Miss Helen Waddell, the Rev. F. Luke Wiseman, Sir Richard Terry, Mr. J. A. Fuller-Maitland, for permission to use the quotations which are specifically acknowledged in their places; to *The Musical Times*, *The Choir*, and the other sources of help detailed in the *Handbook*; to Professor R. A. S. Macalister; and, last but not least, to the Rev. William T. Cairns, D.D., for placing his numerous notes at the editor's disposal, and for unfailing encouragement and help.

EDINBURGH,
May, 1935.

SUPPLEMENTARY NOTES ON HYMNS AND TUNES

INTRODUCTIONS.—To the Third Introduction (The Story of the Revision) the initials M.P.—W.T.C. should be appended.

10 THE SPACIOUS FIRMAMENT ON HIGH

Thackeray's comment on this hymn, in the lecture on Congreve and Addison in *The English Humourists*, deserves quotation: 'When this man looks from the world, whose weaknesses he describes so benevolently, up to the Heaven which shines over us all, I can hardly fancy a human face lighted up with a more serene rapture: a human intellect thrilling with a purer love and adoration than Joseph Addison's. Listen to him: from your childhood you have known the verses: but who can hear their sacred music without love and awe? . . . It seems to me those verses shine like the stars. They shine out of a great deep calm. When he turns to Heaven, a Sabbath comes over that man's mind: and his face lights up from it with a glory of thanks and prayer.'

The tune FIRMAMENT is one of four tunes composed by Sir Walford Davies for the London Church Choir Association for their Festival in St. Paul's in 1908.

11 LET US WITH A GLADSOME MIND

In the Countess of Huntingdon's chapel at Bath, for which Milgrove wrote HARTS, the men and women sat apart on different sides of the building. This facilitated the carrying out of the anti-phonal arrangement of the second part of the tune (see the *Handbook* note) and the instruction given with it: 'The Men that sing the Air must rest where 'tis written the Women to sing this part alone, and begin where the word Altogether is written.'

MELLING in its original form, as set to 'Children of the heavenly King', has the first three lines exactly as in the *Hymnary*, but then proceeds as follows, line 4 being repeated:

12 IMMORTAL, INVISIBLE, GOD ONLY WISE

This hymn had been published seventeen years before it was set to music. The credit of being the first to introduce it into church use belongs to W. Garrett Horder, who included it in his *Congregational Hymns* in 1884.

The tune JOANNA, known also as ST. DENIO, though it has been ascribed to John Roberts of Henllan, is a Welsh traditional secular melody, belonging to a song about the cuckoo, 'Y Gog Lwydlas,' or 'Y Gwcw', and another, 'Can Mlynedd i 'Nawr' (A hundred years from now). The tune has many relatives in English folk-song, one of which is also called 'The Cuckoo'. The *Welsh Folk-Song Journal* prints an early form which appears in the Jenkins Keri MSS. (written about the end of the eighteenth or beginning of the nineteenth century) as 'Rowlands' or 'Can Mlynedd i 'Nawr':

See the *Welsh Folk-Song Journal*, vol. i, pt. iii (1911), pp. 125-8, for variants and notes.

JOANNA as a hymn-tune, first printed as such in 1839, used to be sung, like 'Crug-y-bar' (H. 596), in this form, lengthening the second beat of the bar thus:

(See *Canadiau y Cyssegr*, Denbigh, 1878.)

This apparently syncopated form is a mannerism which seems to have been due to the singing, in Welsh chapels, of triple-time tunes in very slow time, with a pause on the third note of each short phrase.

13 ALL CREATURES OF OUR GOD AND KING

Ozanam, in *Les Poètes Franciscains*, tells how Francis had spent forty nights in his vigils, and had an ecstasy, at the conclusion of which he desired Brother Leo to take a pen and to write, upon which he chanted the Canticle of the Sun. After he had thus improvised, he charged Brother Pacifico, who in the world had been a poet, to reduce the words into a rhythm more exact, and commanded that the brethren should learn them by heart in order to recite them every day.

The original hymn consisted of verses 1 to 4. Verse 5 was occasioned by a quarrel between the Bishop of Assisi and the magistrates. 'The bishop', says Ozanam, 'had put the town under an interdict, and the magistrates in their turn had outlawed the bishop and forbidden all intercourse with him and his.' Francis was deeply affected by this quarrel; and finding that nobody stepped in to interfere, he himself took up his newly-found weapon. He added another verse to the canticle, and 'commanded his disciples to go boldly and seek the great people of the town, and beg them to meet at the bishop's palace.' The name of Francis was so potent that the surprised and reluctant burghers obeyed, not knowing what communication might be about to be made to them. . . . But when the song, with its new verse, fell on their ears, their hearts smote them. 'At the sound of these words, to which God seemed to have lent a gentle strength, the adversaries repented and embraced, and asked each other's pardon.'

Another verse was added to the song a little later, when Francis, weak and suffering, worn out by his great labours and suffering from many bodily afflictions, his eyes so worn that he could scarcely see, his strength reduced by perpetual attacks of fever, after a temporary rally, had a vision from which he learned that in two years his sufferings should be over, and he should enter into eternal rest. Then once more in the joy of his heart he sent for Brother Leo, and added to the song . . . the following and final verse: 'Praised be my Lord by our sister the death of the body' (verses 6 and 7 in Dr. Draper's paraphrase).

'The poem of St. Francis', says Ozanam, 'is very short, and yet all his soul is to be found there—his fraternal friendship for the creatures, the charity which impels a man so humble and gentle to interfere in public quarrels, and that infinite love which, after having sought God in Nature, and served Him in the person of suffering humanity, desires nothing more than to find Him in death. . . . It is nothing but a cry; but it is the cry of a new-born poetry, destined to grow and make itself heard through the whole earth.'

Mrs. Oliphant, from whose *Francis of Assisi* these passages are taken, remarks that 'these quaint and unskilled rhymes' (of the *Cantico del Sole* or *Cantico delle Creature*) 'were the first beginning of vernacular poetry in Italy. . . . It was the faltering tones of the first essay, the hesitating, broken speech of a beginner who is doubtful how far his words will serve him or whether the language is equal to the call he is making upon it.'

Dr. Draper's paraphrase was written for a school-children's Whitsuntide Festival at Leeds, he being then rector of Adel, a few miles away; the precise year is forgotten.

15 LET ALL THE WORLD IN EVERY CORNER SING

Herbert did not write his hymns for congregational singing. Even this one was meant for reading. Yet the fact that he entitled it 'Antiphon' shows that he felt that it ought to be sung; he intended a chorus to sing, 'Let all the world in every corner sing, My God and King!'

17 FOR THE BEAUTY OF THE EARTH

Much objection has been taken to the phrase 'Christ, our God' in the refrain. In some hymn-books it is altered to 'Father, unto Thee'. Mr. Pierpoint answered a correspondent who raised this objection, thus: 'Pliny in his letter to the Emperor said that Christians, when meeting for worship, sang a hymn to Christ as God. As the only public service of the Church was the daily Eucharist, I addressed my hymn to "Christ, our God".'

20 GOD, WHO MADE THE EARTH

First printed in *The Methodist Sunday-School Hymn Book* (1879).

23 SING TO THE LORD A JOYFUL SONG

GONFALON ROYAL was so named because it was written for the hymn 'Vexilla regis prodeunt' ('The royal banners forward go'). A gonfalon is a banner with streamers. Dr. Buck wrote the tune for use in Harrow School, where he was Director of Music.

26 WHEN ALL THY MERCIES, O MY GOD

This hymn comes at the close of an essay on 'Gratitude' in *The Spectator* for August 9, 1712. The subject was congenial to the mind of Addison, of whom Macaulay, in his essay on 'The Life and Writings of Addison', remarks: 'The piety of Addison was of a singularly cheerful character. The feeling which predominates in all his devotional writings is gratitude. . . . On that goodness to which he ascribed all the happiness of his life he relied in the hour of death with the love that casteth out fear.'

Addison, earlier in the essay which the hymn concluded, commented on the curious failure of Christian poets to celebrate adequately the praise of Almighty God. There are few hymns of pure adoration, and every hymn-book shows that the number of great objective hymns to God is very limited. Addison says: 'Most of the works of the pagan poets were either direct hymns to their deities, or tended indirectly to the celebration of their respective attributes and perfections. . . . One would wonder that more of our Christian poets have not turned their thoughts this way, especially if we consider, that our idea of the Supreme Being is not only infinitely more great and noble than what could possibly enter into the heart of an heathen, but filled with everything that can raise the imagination, and give an opportunity for the sublimest thoughts and conceptions.'

31 GOD MOVES IN A MYSTERIOUS WAY

'The tune COLESHILL', says J. A. Fuller-Maitland, 'is nothing more than our English WINDSOR (DUNDEE) translated into the Pentatonic scale.' The musical editor of *Songs of Praise Discussed* says

4

of it: 'It is a magnificent tune, and, in its present version, possibly the greatest of all psalm-tunes.'

Another old form of it is to be found in the MS. psalm-book (1709) of Nicholas Reay, curate of Cumwhitton, near Carlisle, 1711–18. It is there called 'Boulton Tune':

Another traditional variant was used by a 'whole race of sextons' in another Cumberland village to the verse 'Thou turnest man, O Lord, to dust' (from Tate and Brady's Psalm xc. v. 3), sung unaccompanied from the lych-gate to the church:

(See *Transactions*, N.S. xxvi, pp. 334–6, of the Cumberland and Westmorland Antiquarian and Archaeological Society.)

36 ETERNAL LIGHT! ETERNAL LIGHT!

NEWCASTLE was not written by H. K. Morley, but by Henry L. Morley. Mr. Edwin Moss, one of the editors of *The London Tune Book* (1875), for which the tune was written and in which it first appeared, wrote as follows in 1905 to the Rev. Carey Bonner: 'The tune . . . was written by Henry L. Morley at my request. I named it "Newcastle", that being Dr. Binney's birthplace. I knew Mr. Morley by repute as an able musician and an excellent organist. My acquaintance was not a personal one. I have made frequent attempts to obtain information respecting him, but without result. Possibly Mr. Killick Morley (if alive) could help you.' There were thus two Henry Morleys, with different middle names. About neither does much that is definite seem now to be known.

38 SONGS OF PRAISE THE ANGELS SANG

The tune MONKLAND is first found in *Hymn Tunes of the United Brethren* (1824), edited by John Lees, in which the alto and tenor parts are printed on separate staves. Lees was organist of a congregation of the United Brethren (Moravians) at Leominster. This is three miles from Monkland, where John Wilkes was organist, who arranged the tune for the use of Sir Henry Baker, his vicar, in *Hymns Ancient and Modern*, in 1861.

In Lees's book no indication of sources is given, but nearly all his tunes are German chorales. The supposition that MONKLAND might have been derived from a chorale also was confirmed by Dr. W. H. Grattan Flood, who found the source of it in J. A. Freylinghausen's *Geistreiches Gesangbuch* (Hamburg, 1704), in the tune 'Fahre fort'. This tune, which Zahn treats of in his monumental *Die Melodien* (p. 4791), is as follows:

It is obvious that this tune, halved, is transmuted into MONKLAND as it is given in Lees's book:

Note should be taken also of the similarity between FAHRE FORT and LÜBECK (Hymn 170), which was composed by Freylinghausen.

44 LITTLE CHILDREN, WAKE AND LISTEN

In *School Worship* (Congregational Union, 1926) this hymn is credited to Samuel Smith (1771–1835), but authority for this has not been obtainable.

CHARTRES is certainly not later than the middle of the fifteenth century. See *Oxford Book of Carols*, p. 189.

45 THE FIRST NOWELL THE ANGEL DID SAY

The tune is believed to have originally been the treble part (above the melody) of a tune by Jeremiah Clark to 'An Hymn for Christmas Day', which is an elaborated form of ST. MAGNUS. See *Folk-Song Journal*, vol. v, pp. 240–2.

46 HARK! THE HERALD ANGELS SING

Charles Wesley wrote:

> Hark, how all the welkin rings,
> 'Glory to the King of kings!'

This is much closer to the words of Scripture: 'And suddenly there was with the angel [the 'herald angel'] a multitude of the heavenly host, praising God.' The 1904 edition of *Hymns Ancient and Modern* restored 'welkin', but the outcry against it was one of the causes of the non-success of that notable edition.

47 IT CAME UPON THE MIDNIGHT CLEAR

Though it appeared in December, 1850, this hymn had been written in the latter part of the previous year, a time of extraordinary unrest throughout the world, caused by the aftermath of revolution in France and Germany and of the Chartist movement in Great Britain, and in America the passing of the Fugitive Slave Law, and the great 'forty-niner' gold rush to California. The reflection of these occurrences may be traced in vv. 3–5. The American Civil War followed within ten years.

The first half of NOEL is an old English carol-tune, of which various traditional versions are known, which were sung to 'Righteous Joseph', to 'Dives and Lazarus', and to the Sussex carol:

> A glorious angel from Heaven came
> Unto the Virgin Maid,
> Strange news and tidings of great joy
> The humble Mary had.

52 LOVE CAME DOWN AT CHRISTMAS

First appeared in *Time Flies: a Reading Diary* (1885), where the last line, altered in the last edition, was, 'Love the universal sign.'

53 CHILD IN THE MANGER

Between vv. 1 and 2 the original has:

> Monarchs have tender
> Delicate children,
> Nourished in splendour,
> Proud and gay;
> Death soon shall banish
> Honour and beauty,
> Pleasure shall vanish,
> Forms decay.

> *But* the most holy . . .

In the *Hymnary* version this contrast is lost.

54 CHRISTIANS, AWAKE, SALUTE THE HAPPY MORN

Byrom asked his daughter one day what she would like for a Christmas present. She answered, 'Please write me a poem.' When she came down to breakfast on Christmas Day, 1749, she found on her plate a sheet with this hymn on it, headed, 'Christmas Day for Dolly.' The original MS. is preserved in the Chetham Library, Manchester. Considerable changes, all improvements, were made on the first draft by the author before he published the hymn in his *Poems, &c.* 1773.

The form in which the tune is given in John Wainwright's own *Collection* is in two parts, soprano and bass, with the bass figured; but at the words 'Of God Incarnate and the Virgin's Son' the music is in four parts and headed 'Chorus'. This probably accounts for the West Riding custom of repeating the last strain of the tune as a chorus.

55 O COME, ALL YE FAITHFUL

In the Preface (p. x) to *The Hundred Best Latin Hymns* Prof. J. S. Phillimore said: 'It is not impossible that we have in it the remains of a medieval Christmas Sequence from some manuscript that was lost in the ravaging of libraries at the Reformation.' This, however, is conjecture.

58 GOOD CHRISTIAN MEN, REJOICE

A *patois* carol, perhaps of the fourteenth century, from *Carols for Christmastide*, by Rev. Thomas Helmore and Rev. J. M. Neale. In the Preface to the first edition (1853) Neale said: 'It will be sufficient to observe that, scattered over the whole of medieval Europe, there were a certain number of these compositions—the ground-work of words and music being the same; but certain national peculiarities, in the course of ages, finding their way into both. They belong, exclusively, to no one portion of the Western Church—though one carol might be more popular here, and another there. They were generally in Latin—often had a vernacular translation—and were sometimes composed in a *patois* of the two.'

60 OF THE FATHER'S LOVE BEGOTTEN

In an article on Prudentius in *The Church Quarterly Review* for July 1928, Dr. Alex. Nairne, Regius Professor of Divinity, Cambridge, says: 'The fact is that Prudentius is not a writer of hymns. He is called so, for he is popularly known through hymn-books. Extracts were made from his long poems and were put into Latin breviaries. The very ancient Spanish or Mozarabic Breviary has many of these, and sometimes considerable liberties have been taken with the text. These hymns, more or less faithfully representing him, have been made out of Prudentius. But at their best they spoil him. The length, the elbow-room, as of an out-door landscape, are characteristic. What he wrote were poems, to be read—not always aloud—in the study, the garden, on the mountain or by the river; a prayer-book, but a poet's—a book of meditations, not of Church offices.'

63 AS WITH GLADNESS MEN OF OLD
Chatterton Dix wrote this while lying ill, on the Epiphany, *c.* 1858, after reading the Gospel for the day.

64 BRIGHTEST AND BEST OF THE SONS OF THE MORNING
Heber wrote this hymn for the Scots tune 'Wandering Willie'. See Introduction, p. xxix.

65 ANGELS FROM THE REALMS OF GLORY
LLANDINAM appeared under the name ERPINGHAM in *The People's Music Book*, Pt. I, edited by James Turle and Edward Taylor (London, 1848). It was there given anonymously.

68 THERE CAME A LITTLE CHILD TO EARTH
'My simple little CHILDREN'S SONG was expressly written for the Earl (afterwards Marquess) of Aberdeen, for his children to sing on Christmas morning, 1890.' (Note by Mr. Walton in *The Book of Common Praise* of the Episcopal Church of Canada.)

70 COME, PRAISE YOUR LORD AND SAVIOUR
A version of GOSTERWOOD noted by the late Dr. Clague in the Isle of Man as a 'carval' (ballad-carol) tune is printed in W. H. Gill's *Manx National Music*, p. 87. It was also sung to the early Primitive Methodist hymn, 'Come, all ye weary travellers,' and appears as late as *c.* 1895 in the P.M. *Mission Hymnal* to 'Gospel News'. It seems to have been an old tune to which 'When the stormy winds do blow' was sung.

74 O SING A SONG OF BETHLEHEM
The melody named KINGSFOLD is a widely spread folk-tune whose proper name seems to be 'Come all you worthy Christians', from the old ballad-carol beginning thus, to which it used to be sung. The particular version called KINGSFOLD by Dr. Vaughan Williams is based on the variant noted by A. J. Hipkins in Westminster, without words, but under the name of 'Lazarus'. The 'Dives and Lazarus' carol with which it was associated is printed with Mr. Hipkins' tune in *English County Songs* (1893) edited by Miss Lucy E. Broadwood and J. A. Fuller Maitland, from which it was reproduced in *The English Hymnal* and *The Church Hymnary*, but the tune has been used also by folk-singers for other ballads of a tragic or melancholy cast. For various other versions and references see

9

The Folk-Song Journal, vol. ii, pp. 115–23, under the heading 'Come, all ye faithful Christians'. Dr. Vaughan Williams found one of the versions he noted at Kingsfold, Surrey, whence his name for the tune; but there is no doubt that the carol is earlier than 'Maria Martin', the Kingsfold ballad. Miss Broadwood traces a likeness between this air and the tune of the old Scottish ballad 'Gilderoy'.

76 BEHOLD A LITTLE CHILD

LOVE UNKNOWN was contributed by John Ireland to *The Public School Hymn Book* (1919).

WESLEY is founded on the undernoted melody, named 'David' in *The Wesleyan Sunday School Tune Book* (1858), where it is said to be by Handel. Apparently it was adapted from an air in Handel's opera *Sosarme*.

81 GOD WHO HATH MADE THE DAISIES

The carol-melody of ES IST EIN ROS' ENTSPRUNGEN is believed to have belonged to an older Christmas or Twelfth Night carol, used in the diocese of Trier or Trèves, the ancient Augusta Trevirorum, which claims to be the oldest town in Germany. The title ('A rose has bloomed') uses the image of a rose come forth from 'the stem of Jesse', and applies it to Mary the mother of the child.

The melody in its proper form has a tune of seven lines, and is as follows:

84 FIERCE WAS THE WILD BILLOW

'Congregations used to be puzzled by the "wail of Euroclydon" in verse 2. Who was Euroclydon? Only a learned blunder of Neale's. St. Mark does not make the mistake of calling the fierce local squalls on the lake of Galilee by this name. The "euroclydon" or "euraquilo" is indeed mentioned in Acts xxvii. 14; but it was a north-east wind from the mountains of Crete. "Euros" is the south-east wind, and "aquilo" the north wind, so that "euraquilo" was probably a sailor's name for a local "tempestuous wind" such as buffeted the ship of St. Paul off Cape Matala.'—*Songs of Praise Discussed*.

91 ALL GLORY, LAUD, AND HONOUR.

The legend that Louis the Pious, on Palm Sunday, 821, hearing Theodulph sing the original of this hymn at the window of his prison at Angers, released the bishop, restored him to his see, and ordained that thenceforth the hymn was always to be sung in processions on Palm Sunday, cannot possibly be true, since Louis was never in Angers after 818, and Theodulph almost certainly never had his see restored. Yet it is a fact that soon after the good bishop's time the hymn came into use in the Palm Sunday procession in France and England. According to the Sarum use the first four verses were to be sung before leaving the church by seven boys in a high place near the south door. In the use of York a temporary gallery was provided over the door of the church from which the boys of the choir sang the first four stanzas. After each of the first three stanzas the rest of the choir, kneeling below, sang ver. 1 as refrain. At the end of ver. 4 the boys began the refrain and the rest of the choir stood up and sang it with them. In many places the full thirty-nine verses would be none too many for the requirements, for the Hereford use provided that the procession should go to the gates of the city, and, that the gates being shut, seven choir-boys should mount to the top of the gate-house and there sing. The uses of Tours and Rouen also required it to be sung at the gate of the city.

The theory that the tune is an adaptation of the famous sixteenth-century air and dance known as 'Sellinger's Round', though the editor of *The Oxford Hymn Book* (1920) has the courage to advance it as a fact, is fantastic.

A setting of the chorale by Bach will be found in *The Church Anthem Book*.

97 O WORD OF PITY, FOR OUR PARDON PLEADING

The supposition that PSALM 80 might be of Scottish origin is now known to be untenable. The tune is found in the *Piae Cantiones* (1582) (see pp. 458–9 of *Handbook*). It made its appearance in Scotland earlier (1564). But Woodward, in his reprint of the *Piae Cantiones*, says: 'For the earliest form [of this tune] see the Hohen-furth MS. (*Graduale Altovadense* of 1410), as given in *Analecta Hymnica*, I. Anhang, No. ix, p. 92; see Zahn, No. 1576, Meister I, No. 278.' He states also that the *Piae Cantiones* air has been harmonized by fourteen musicians (amongst others) whose names he gives, from Johann Walther in 1524 to J. S. Bach, both in his 371 *Vierstimmige Choral-Gesänge* (No. 30) and in his *Organ Works*;

and that it appears in 1854 in *The Hymnal Noted*, there set to English words beginning 'In our common celebration' (Neale's translation of 'Omnes una celebremus'). 'But to accommodate the tune of "Jesus Christus nostra salus" (as in the *Piae Cantiones*) to words of a different metre, unpardonable liberties were taken with it.'

100 THRONED UPON THE AWFUL TREE

ARFON, though arranged from a Welsh melody, appears to have been derived from a French original; at any rate it is given in R. Guilmant's *Noëls* (1885) as the traditional melody to the carol 'Joseph est bien marié'; and in G. Legeay's *Noëls Anciens* (1875) to 'Un nouveau présent des Cieux', in a slightly simpler form.

The Welsh form appears, according to the Rev. James Mearns, to be taken from a folk-song *Tros y Garreg* (Over the stone), in Edward Jones's *Welsh Bards*, 1794. There seem to be two tunes of this name, 'Meribah' being an alternative title for this one, whose metre is given by W. S. Gwynn Williams (*Welsh National Music and Dance*) as 87.87 Double.

102 O PERFECT LIFE OF LOVE

The subject of the tune SOUTHWELL is identical with that of Tallis's sequence motet 'Absterge, Domine', in the *Cantiones Sacrae* (1578).

106 WHEN I SURVEY THE WONDROUS CROSS

The tune TUNBRIDGE referred to in the note on ROCKINGHAM (COMMUNION) leaves no doubt as to its being the proximate source from which Dr. Miller acknowledged having taken part of his melody; his own copy of the tune exists, with a note in his handwriting, 'would make a good Long M[etre].' See facsimile in *The Musical Times*, May 1909, p. 314.

But TUNBRIDGE appears, fairly clearly, to have been itself derived from some earlier source. The crotchets at the beginning of the bars in the 2nd, 3rd, and 4th lines are palpably split minims, showing that the tune has been adapted to fit the words—'All ye that pass by, To Jesus draw nigh'—to which it is set in the book where it is found, Aaron Williams's *Psalmody in Miniature* (1778 onwards), which Mr. J. T. Lightwood calls a 'minified form' of Williams's *Universal Psalmodist*.

Miss A. G. Gilchrist draws attention to the melody of 'The Bonie Banks of Ayr' in the *Miniature Museum of Scottish Song* (*c.* 1810), as showing in several of its phrases a remarkable resemblance to this tune.

The name ROCKINGHAM was given to the tune by Dr. Miller 'in grateful memory of the Marquis of Rockingham, his kind and zealous patron and honoured lord'. Rockingham was Prime Minister in 1765–6 and 1782; in the latter year he died.

108 SING, MY TONGUE, HOW GLORIOUS BATTLE

The relic of the true Cross referred to in the note on this hymn was set in a gold triptych enriched with enamel and inlaid with precious stones; part of it is still treasured at Poitiers in the present Convent of the Holy Cross. It is described as a small gold panel, covered with a scroll design in cloisonné enamel, and a cruciform cavity in the middle contains the wood.

Miss Helen Waddell says in her *Medieval Latin Lyrics* (pp. 301–2): 'There was no grossness in Fortunatus, and there were times when fire was laid upon his lips. . . . If he loved good cheer, he loved goodness more; and he had as absolute a vision as that older materialist and mystic, of the ladder between earth and heaven.' In her fine book on *The Wandering Scholars* also (p. 26) she says: 'Both "Vexilla Regis" and the other, "Pange lingua gloriosi", are a mystic's Dream of the Rood. It is not as the Latins took it, the symbol and the sign: to Fortunatus, it is still the tree as it grew in the forest, foredoomed to its great and terrible destiny.'

'Fortunatus was the chief representative of literature in Gaul in the sixth century,' says E. L. F. Veitch in *The Church Quarterly Review* for October, 1929. 'The man who wrote "Vexilla Regis" and "Pange lingua" had in him the gift of expression approaching the quality of creation, able to suggest things beyond perception. . . . To Fortunatus the Cross is the *spes unica* of the world, and it is in his poems on the subject and in his hymns that we realize his passionate piety, his Christian mysticism, his capacity for deep religious experience and emotion. . . . His hymns will for ever rank among the most precious possessions of the Church.'

110 AND CAN IT BE, THAT I SHOULD GAIN

F. Luke Wiseman, in his *Charles Wesley, Evangelist and Poet* (p. 76), says of this hymn: 'Note especially the last two verses in which, using the figure of his oft-quoted Galatians passage, he represents himself as "concluded"—that is, shut up, or as we might say, "locked up", for his sin, like the poor denizens of Newgate Jail he so often visited. Weaving in with this the details of the story of Peter in prison on the night before his expected execution, Wesley dramatically describes his own condition in verse—"Long my imprisoned spirit lay".'

The tune to which this hymn is set in the *Collection of Tunes, set to Music, as they are commonly Sung at the Foundery*, issued by John Wesley in 1742, for use in the old state cannon-foundry which Charles Wesley bought in 1739 as the site of the first Methodist meeting-house in London, is LAMBETH or CRUCIFIXION, by S. Akeroyd (published in *The Divine Companion*, 1722). See *The English Hymnal*, 340, and *The Methodist Hymn Book* (1933), 28 in Additional Tunes. A note in the latter book says: 'There is strong reason to believe that this is the tune sung by John Wesley on the night of his conversion, May 24, 1738.'

119 JESUS CHRIST IS RISEN TO-DAY

For another old version of EASTER HYMN, with a different distribution of the words, see *The Musical Times*, April 1904.

122 THE STRIFE IS O'ER, THE BATTLE DONE

Sir Richard Terry, in an essay on 'The Genesis of a Popular Hymn-Tune' in his *On Music's Borders*, offers strong objection to the tune VICTORY being ascribed to Palestrina. It is an adaptation from the *Gloria* of Palestrina's *Magnificat Tertii Toni* (1591), which is as follows:

Sir Richard thus criticizes Monk's treatment of 'this perfectly constructed, beautifully balanced, and delicately poised little gem, first destroying its modal character, secondly destroying its rhythm, and finally mauling its harmonies about, till *only one bar* (the thirteenth) remains as Palestrina wrote it. . . . Even when he does get his chords in the same position as Palestrina's, he alters the value of the notes. And yet "in quires and places where they sing", Doctor Monk's grotesque perversion is still quoted as an example of Palestrina's style.' Upon this Sir Richard not unreasonably pleads that in future VICTORY should bear Monk's name alone.

Probably the earliest English hymn-tune constructed from Palestrina's *Gloria Patri* is the adaptation in *The Parish Choir* (1846–51), where it is set to the hymn 'Come, Holy Ghost, our souls inspire'. As W. H. Monk was the anonymous editor of that collection, this earlier adaptation was doubtless by him also. It bears, as will be seen below, a closer relation than VICTORY to the original:

There is a reminiscence of Palestrina's melody in Dowland's 'Floodis of Teares' in Forbes's Aberdeen *Cantus* (1662). Can some echo of 'Floodis of Teares' have suggested the use of the Scottish 8.6.8.6. form of the tune PALESTRINA for penitential psalms?

123 THE DAY OF RESURRECTION

This is the first of the eight odes of *The Golden Canon* or *Queen of Canons*, by John of Damascus, which is sung in the Eastern Church after midnight on Easter morning, to set forth the fact of the resurrection, its fulfilment of the prophecies, and the benefits it has brought mankind, and to call the people to thanksgiving and praise. In the preface to his *Hymns of the Eastern Church* Neale quotes an eloquent description of a typical service in Athens on Easter morning, at which the canon was sung. The passage is given also in Julian's *Dictionary of Hymnology*, p. 62. The people assemble in the darkened church, with unlighted tapers in their hands, and while the priests chant in a half-whisper, they await the signal that Easter Day has begun. A cannon is fired when the moment comes, and on the instant the Cross is raised with the cry 'Christos anesti, Christ is risen'. The multitude take up the exultant cry, the tapers are lighted, and the dark church is filled with a blaze of light. Outside, drums beat and trumpets sound, and people, meeting, embrace and congratulate one another with beaming faces, repeating the salutation, 'Christ is risen'. In Russia in the old days even the Tsar as he left his palace on Easter morning would kiss the sentry at the gate as he gave him the salutation 'Christ is risen'.

124 O SONS AND DAUGHTERS, LET US SING

The melody O FILII ET FILIAE has been found in seventeenth- as well as eighteenth-century collections, the first so far being *Airs sur les hymnes sacrez, odes et noëls* (Paris, 1673). It is of the second mode, and is probably an adaptation of a French traditional melody.

125 OUR LORD CHRIST HATH RISEN

This hymn was specially written for the Irish *Church Hymnal* in order to make it possible to include the tune there fitted to it.

130 THE GOLDEN GATES ARE LIFTED UP

An earlier form of this hymn, 'The eternal gates lift up their heads', appeared in the S.P.C.K. *Hymns* (1852), and is still in use.

131 THE HEAD THAT ONCE WAS CROWNED WITH THORNS

In line 5 of the note, for *second* read *third* edition: see *The Musical Times*, January 1906.

135 REJOICE, THE LORD IS KING

The story of Handel's tune GOPSAL is interesting. The owner of Covent Garden theatre in the middle of the eighteenth century was John Rich, who invented the pantomime, was himself known as 'the prince of harlequins', and was the producer of *The Beggar's Opera*, of which a popular quip said that 'it made Gay rich and Rich gay'. His wife, herself an actress, was converted under Charles Wesley's preaching, and renounced the stage; when her husband insisted on her returning to it, she declared that she would only go back to bear her testimony against it. Handel taught her daughters, and it was doubtless at her request that he wrote tunes for three of Charles Wesley's hymns, her own favourites probably. The tunes were: GOPSAL, to this hymn; CANNONS (see note on the tune in Notes on Psalter Tunes in this Supplement), originally called 'The Invitation' because of its being written for the hymn 'Sinners, obey the Gospel word'; and FITZWILLIAM, then called 'Desiring to Love', because of its being set to 'O Love Divine, how sweet thou art'. The date of their composition is uncertain, but it must have been between 1749, when two of the hymns first appeared, and 1752, when Handel's eyesight was rapidly failing.

The subsequent fortunes of the tunes are uncertain. They seem to have remained in private possession, for none of them appeared in any of the books for the use of Methodists in the eighteenth century. Nor did any of them appear in print till over seventy years after Handel's death. By a remarkable coincidence they were discovered in 1826, in Handel's autograph, probably on the very slip of paper on which he had written them for Mrs. Rich, by Samuel Wesley, Charles's son, the composer. He had obtained a Grace from the University of Cambridge authorizing him to transcribe and publish any of the valuable musical MSS. in the library of the Fitzwilliam Museum, and there the treasure was found. Samuel described the style of the tunes as 'alike simple, solemn, and easy of execution to all who can sing or play a plain Psalm tune'. He believed that these 'Relicks of Piety' deserved publication, and in January, 1827, they were advertised in *The Wesleyan Methodist Magazine* as follows:

'The FITZWILLIAM MUSIC, never before published: *Three Hymns*: the words by the late Rev. Charles Wesley, A.M., of Christ Church College, Oxford; and set to music by George Frederick Handel, faithfully transcribed from his Autography in the Library of the Fitzwilliam Museum, Cambridge, by Samuel Wesley, and now very respectfully promoted to the Wesleyan Society at large. Price 1s. 6d.'

A photograph of the autograph MS. is given in the annotated edition of *The Book of Common Praise* of the Canadian Episcopal Church, and also in *The Choir* for May, 1930. From articles by Mr. J. T. Lightwood in the March and May numbers of that magazine for 1930, these particulars are taken.

In Whit-week of 1773 a new organ was opened in Walsall Parish Church. The service on the occasion closed with the 148th Psalm to a new tune by the vicar. This was the tune that bears his name, DARWALL. It had appeared three years previously in Williams's *New Universal Psalmodist*. It was for Tate and Brady's (New)

Version of the Psalter that Darwall wrote his 150 tunes, one for each psalm. A facsimile of Darwall's MS. of the present tune is given in the Historical Edition (1904) of *Hymns Ancient and Modern*, p. xcviii. This shows that the first note, as he wrote the tune, was A, thus:

144 AND DIDST THOU LOVE THE RACE THAT LOVED NOT THEE?

Miss Ingelow's poem is on 'The Love of Christ'. The credit of making the cento from it belongs to *The Congregational Church Hymnal* of 1887.

146 O SON OF MAN, OUR HERO STRONG AND TENDER

Written for Charterhouse about 1924, and used in the school for some time before it was published. The tune sung to it there is by Mr. R. S. Thatcher.

149 O COME, O COME, IMMANUEL

The Greater Antiphons, sung at Vespers from Dec. 17 each evening till Christmas Eve, began as follows:

> O Sapientia, quae ex ore altissimi.
> O Adonay et dux domus Israel.
> O Radix Jesse qui stas in signum populorum.
> O Clavis David et sceptrum domus Israel.
> O Oriens, splendor lucis aeternae.
> O Rex gentium et desideratus.
> O Emanuel, rex et legifer noster.

It is easy to observe which five of these were selected by the unknown writer of the twelfth or thirteenth century to be woven into the Latin hymn which Neale translated. Neale's first version began, 'Draw nigh, draw nigh, Emmanuel', in his *Medieval Hymns* (1851); but two years later, in *The Hymnal Noted*, he altered this to the well-known form.

153 'THY KINGDOM COME!'—ON BENDED KNEE

Dr. Hosmer's hymn first appeared in the second series of his *The Thought of God* (1894). Its first appearance in Great Britain was in Garrett Horder's *Worship Song* (1905), *The English Hymnal* coming next in 1906.

The Dublin *Collection of Hymns and Sacred Poems* (1749) in which IRISH made its first appearance is sometimes claimed for John Wesley. He was certainly in Dublin in that year, and J. F. Lampe (q.v.) was with him; the supposition is that Lampe edited the music of the collection for him. There is nothing characteristically Irish about the tune, but neither does it exhibit the qualities of Lampe's usual work.

154 HAIL TO THE LORD'S ANOINTED

The original form of CRÜGER was as follows:

In late editions of his *Praxis Pietatis Melica* the second line runs:

Variants have been numerous, but W. H. Monk's adaptation of it for *Hymns Ancient and Modern*, with line 5 of his own composition, has greatly improved the tune and probably settled its form for use with the English language.

155 MINE EYES HAVE SEEN THE GLORY OF THE COMING OF THE LORD

This hymn was written to be sung to the tune of 'John Brown's body lies a-mouldering in the grave'. John Brown (1800–59), as became a scion of Pilgrim Fathers' stock, was a man of intense religious convictions and heroic and self-sacrificing courage. He became in boyhood a passionate abolitionist. After years of apparently useless pleading and struggle for the emancipation of the slaves, he resolved in 1859 to force the Government to take action. In October of that year, with nineteen men, he seized the Government arsenal at Harper's Ferry, Virginia, with a view to starting a widespread uprising of the slaves. The attempt failed. Brown was arrested, tried, and executed at Charlestown on Dec. 2. Before the attack on the arsenal he had said, 'If we lose our lives, it will perhaps do more for the cause than our lives would be worth in any other way.' He went to the scaffold, an observer said, 'with a radiant countenance and the step of a conqueror'. In a striking poem written before the execution Edmund Clarence Stedman warned the Virginian authorities against proceeding to extremities: 'Old Brown . . . may trouble you more than ever when you've nailed his coffin down.' So it befell. Soon after Brown's death Thoreau wrote: 'Of all the men who were my contemporaries, it seems to me that John Brown is the only one who has not died. I meet him at every turn. He is more alive than ever he was. He is not longer working in secret. He works in public in the clearest light that shines in the land.'

Brown's death aroused the conscience of the North on the subject of emancipation as nothing else had done. It helped also to consolidate the South. Victor Hugo's verdict was: 'What the South slew was not John Brown, but slavery.' A poet had written:

> Not any spot six feet by two
> Can hold a man like thee;
> John Brown shall tramp the shaking earth
> From Blue Ridge to the sea.

This prophecy also was fulfilled. Brown's name became a battle-cry among the armies of the North; they marched to the strains of the doggerel song, which enshrines his heroic memory:

> John Brown's body lies a-mouldering in the grave;
> But his soul is marching on.

One verse in particular expresses the fiery passion his death aroused:

> He captured Harper's Ferry
> With his nineteen men so true,
> And he frightened old Virginia
> Till she trembled through and through;
> They hung him for a traitor,
> Themselves a traitor-crew;
> But his soul is marching on.

Brander Matthews, in an article on 'The Songs of the War' in *The Century Magazine* of Aug. 1887, says that the genesis of both words and music of this song is obscure and involved. 'The martial hymn has been called a spontaneous generation of the uprising of the North—a self-made song, which sang itself into being of its own accord. Some have treated it as a sudden evolution from the inner consciousness of the early soldiers all aglow with free-soil enthusiasm; and these speak of it as springing, like Minerva from the head of Jove, full-armed and mature. Others have more happily likened it to Topsy, in that it never was born, it growed; and this latter theory has the support of the facts as far as they can be disentangled from a maze of fiction and legend.'

The facts appear to be that the song was put together by a quartet of men in the Twelfth Massachusetts Volunteers, and was first adopted as a marching song by that regiment; they first sang it in public as they marched down Broadway, New York, on July 24, 1861, on their way from Boston to the front. The tune which thus passed into national use in association with Brown's name was perfect for its purpose. 'There was a majestic simplicity in the rhythm like the beating of mighty hammers.' Louis Elson, in *The National Music of America* (1900), states that it was originally a hymn-tune. Though claimed by William Steffe, of Philadelphia, a popular Sunday School composer, as his own, it appears to have been a very old Methodist camp-meeting song, said to have been used in Charleston, both in coloured churches and among the firemen, long before the Civil War. The hymn belongs to the improvisatory type, and the soldiers' parody, in improvised lines (no rhymes were required) was of that type also. Elson prints a copy of the hymn-tune 'Say, brothers, will you meet us?' from an old Methodist hymnal 'of about half a century ago' (from 1900). This hymn, as 'Say, brother, will you meet me?' was brought, with its music, to this country by Mr. John Macgregor of the Temple, who asked Dr. E. J. Hopkins to make a four-part arrangement of it, which was published in 1859 for Mr. Edmund Macrory (author of *Notes on the Temple Organ*) and presented by the two Benchers to the Ragged School Shoe-black Society, for whose benefit it was sold. The hymn was sung at the Shoe-blacks' winter treat on February 8, 1859, at St. Martin's Hall. Hymn and tune are found in *Richard Weaver's Tune-Book* (c. 1861–2).

The circumstances in which Mrs. Julia Ward Howe was moved to write the present hymn to the popular air are given in the *Handbook* note, the first sentence of which, however, should read, 'written in December 1861, six months after the outbreak of the American Civil War.' A copy of the hymn, in her autograph, appeared in the article referred to in *The Century Magazine* for 1887, with a portrait of herself and a striking one of John Brown.

From this autograph it appears that Mrs. Howe wrote 'fateful' and 'through the vineyard' in v. 1, and in v. 3, 'let us die to make men free.' The two verses (3 and 4) omitted in the *Hymnary* were as follows:

I have seen Him in the watch-fires of an hundred circling camps;
They have builded Him an altar in the evening dews and damps;
I can read His righteous sentence by the dim and flaring lamps.
    His day is marching on.

I have read a fiery gospel, writ in burnished rows of steel,
'As ye deal with my contemners, so with you my grace shall deal;
Let the hero, born of woman, crush the serpent with his heel,
    Since God is marching on.'

160 LO! HE COMES, WITH CLOUDS DESCENDING

There seems to be little doubt that HELMSLEY is an adaptation of a popular eighteenth-century air, known variously as 'De'il tak' the wars that hurried Billy frae me', 'Guardian Angels', and 'Miss Catley's Hornpipe', and used by Sheridan for his song 'When sable night each drooping plant restoring', in *The Duenna*. And so the story that Olivers had heard it whistled in the street can easily be credited. See 'New Light on the Ancestry of *Helmsley*' in *The Choir*, April 1928.

161 THAT DAY OF WRATH, THAT DREADFUL DAY

The 'Dies Irae' was one of the five sequences spared in the holocaust of hymns of that type ordained by the Council of Trent. Originally it was probably an Advent hymn, but it was early taken into use for masses for the dead and for All Souls' Day.

Sir Walter Scott, writing about 1812 to Crabbe, who had been asked by the Rev. A. Brunton, Edinburgh, to 'furnish hymns which had relation to the Old or New Testament', said: 'I think these hymns which do not immediately recall the warm and exalted language of the Bible are apt to be, however elegant, rather cold and flat for purposes of devotion. You will readily believe that I do not approve of the vague and indiscriminate Scripture language which the fanatics of old, and the modern Methodists, have adopted, but merely that solemnity and peculiarity of diction which at once puts the reader on his guard as to the purpose of the poetry. To my Gothic ear, indeed, the *Stabat Mater*, the *Dies Irae*, and some of the other hymns of the Catholic Church, are more solemn and affecting than the fine classical poetry of Buchanan: the one has the gloomy dignity of a Gothic church, and reminds us instantly of the worship to which it is dedicated: the other is more like a Pagan temple, recalling to our memory the classical and fabulous deities.' (Lockhart, *Life of Scott*, vol. ii, p. 240.)

166 O FOR A THOUSAND TONGUES, TO SING

This hymn has stood first in Methodist hymn-books on both sides of the Atlantic for 150 years.

Sydney Dimond, in *The Psychology of the Methodist Revival*, says: 'In the manuscript hymn-book which was Wesley's constant companion on his evangelistic tours . . . the pages which show signs of most frequent use are those where he found

O for a thousand tongues, to sing
My dear Redeemer's praise.'

168 YE SERVANTS OF GOD, YOUR MASTER PROCLAIM

This hymn is No. 1 of 'Hymns to be sung in Tumult' in *Hymns for Times of Trouble and Persecution* (1744).

Parry's magnificent tune, LAUDATE DOMINUM, is an arrangement made by himself from one of his anthems, 'Hear my words, O ye people', which he composed in 1894 for the Festival of the Salisbury Diocesan Festival Association. The music was written for Sir Henry Baker's hymn 'O praise ye the Lord, praise Him in the height', which forms the concluding part of the anthem.

170 SWEETER SOUNDS THAN MUSIC KNOWS

For the tune LÜBECK see note on MONKLAND (Hymn 38) in this Supplement.

The tune from which FESTUS is derived, in Freylinghausen's *Geistreiches Gesangbuch* (Halle, 1704), set to the hymn 'O du Hüter Israels', is as follows:

FESTUS appears sometimes as L.M., sometimes as 77.77, in English tune-books about the sixties or seventies of last century. Whoever made the adaptation spoiled a magnificent tune.

172 O LIGHT, WHOSE BEAMS ILLUMINE ALL

In its original form SURREY was in two parts, treble and figured bass, the melody being as follows:

174 REST OF THE WEARY, JOY OF THE SAD

The tune FORTUNE has a remarkable history. The old Titus Andronicus ballad upon which Shakespeare is said to have founded his play was sung to it. It is mentioned in *The Merry Wives of Windsor*, and was the tune to which scores of ballads, mostly of a melancholy cast, were sung in Elizabethan days and later. It was called the 'Hanging Tune' because lamentations of criminals were sung to it for at least 200 years. In some parts of Scotland MARTYRS was used in a similar way.

FORTUNE was sung in Scotland in the sixteenth century to two of the earliest songs of the Reformation. About the year 1546 there appeared a notable book entitled *Ane Compendious Buik of Godlie Psalmes and Spirituall Sangis*, better known by the briefer name, *The Gude and Godlie Ballatis*, which leapt into widespread favour in Scotland among the middle and trading classes. The authors were three brothers Wedderburn, of Dundee. It contained not only twenty-two psalms in metre, translations into Scots of several Lutheran hymns, and spiritual meditations, but racy satires on the clergy and the Church as it then was.

Among the songs was one, 'Welcum Fortoun'—a simple love-song —which had a curious history. One theory about it is, that it was a purified form of an older and grosser song; another, that it was written by Robert Wedderburn, who was vicar of Dundee, to express his un-dying devotion to the lady of his heart whom his position as a priest made it impossible for him to marry. If the latter theory be correct, it would appear probable that the constancy was on one side only, for another of the ballads is entitled 'My Lufe was fals and ful of flattry', and another still, one of the finest hymns in the book, adapts 'Welcum Fortoun' to the theme of heavenly love, as though the writer's heart-ache made him turn to One whose love would never fail him.

By some unexplained fortune—trick or accident?—the first song found its way into one of the early editions of the Psalm-book, published by Bassandyne. The General Assembly of July 1568 took grave notice of the irregularity, as its records show: 'It was delaitit and found that Thomas Bassandine, Printer in Edinburgh, imprintit . . . ane psalme booke, in the end whereof was found printed ane baudie song called Welcum Fortoun, whilk book he had printed without licence of the magistrate, or reviseing of the Kirk: Therfor the haill Assemblie ordainit the said Thomas to call in againe all the said bookes that he has sauld, and keip the rest un-sauld untill he . . . delete the said baudie song out of the end of the psalm booke. And farther, that he abstaine in all tyme coming from farther printing of anything without licence of the supreame magis-trate, and reviseing of sick things as pertaine to religioun be some of the Kirk appointed for that purpose.'

The edict of the Assembly was so thoroughly carried out that the song in question disappeared from knowledge for 300 years. When Prof. A. F. Mitchell discovered a copy, the Assembly's description of it was found to exceed in severity. A few lines were somewhat free, according to the habit of the time, but in the main the song is accurately described by Prof. J. H. Millar (*The Literary History of Scotland*) as 'a love song of very considerable merit and unimpeachable decency'. Even so, of course, it was ludicrously out of place in the Church's authorized Psalm-book.

Two verses from the later—spiritual—song, sung to the tune FORTUNE, are as follows:

> Welcum, Lord Christ, welcum againe,
>   My joy, my comfort, and my bliss,
> That culd me saif from hellis paine,
>   Bot onlie thow nane was, and is . . .

> Was never nane to me mair kynde
>   Nor Christ; thairfore I will him pryse,
> Onlie with saule, body, and mynde,
>   My hope and traist haill in him lyes.

179 CHRIST IS THE WORLD'S REDEEMER

See Note in *Handbook* on Hymn 454. The tradition is that Columba laboured for seven years, in a dark cell without light, in penance for his famous fight against the High-king Diarmuid at Cooldrevny, on his great hymn ('or rather cosmogonical and eschatological poem', says Mr. Stephen Gaselee, 'though it was used as a hymn in Ireland'), the *Altus Prosator*, so called from its opening words, 'Altus prosator vetustus dierum et ingenitus'. (The Latin text is given by Mr. Gaselee in *The Oxford Book of Medieval Latin Verse*.) When messengers came to Iona from Pope Gregory (the Great) bearing gifts among which was a book of Hymns of the Week which Gregory himself had compiled, Columba gave them his own hymn to take back to the Pope. The latter, acknowledging it, 'said the hymn would be the best of all praises if Colum Cille had not too slightly commended the Trinity *per se*, as well as in Its creatures' (Helen Waddell, *Medieval Latin Lyrics*). Columba, admitting the justice of the criticism, made amends by composing a new hymn to the glory of the Trinity alone: *In Te, Christe, credentium miserearis omnium.* One portion of this, translated, gives us the present hymn; another is found in Hymn 454.

Of part of the *Altus* Prof. R. A. S. Macalister gives the following vigorous rendering:

> Ancient of Days, throned high in majesty,
>   The Father, Holy Spirit, Christ the Son,
> Who wast and art from all eternity
>   In everlasting glory, Three in One,
> Founder of all the worlds, we worship Thee.

> Called into being by the word of might,
>   The angels stood within Thy Holy Place,
> To do Thy will as ministers of light,
>   To bear throughout the furthest bounds of space
> The bounties of Thy goodness infinite.

Then, O Most-Highest, all-foreseeing, fast
  This earth on its foundations didst Thou build,
Yon sky, the seas, the lands upon them cast,
  With waving trees and living creatures filled,
And man, their ruler, fashioned at the last.

The Morning Stars their mighty chorus sang,
  The angels praised Thy wondrous works of power,
Throughout Heav'n's arches the tremendous clang
  Thundered and echoed in that birth-time hour,
And the great anthem thro' the universe rang.

When once again the trumpet-blast shall sound,
  When in the awful Second Advent-Day,
Stars, like ripe fruit, shall rain upon the ground,
  The sun and moon shall fail, and men shall say
'Fall on us' to the rugged cliffs around,

When by the fiery wrath of judgement-sword
  Thine enemies shall perish: but Thy grace
Hath promised us who trust Thee and Thy word,
  We in the air shall meet Thee, face to face—
So shall we be for ever with the Lord.

The original melody of MOVILLE will be found in Petrie, No. 1234, 'Scorching is this love'.

182 COME, HOLY GHOST, OUR SOULS INSPIRE

184 CREATOR SPIRIT! BY WHOSE AID

It is unfortunate that the creative idea in *Veni, Creator Spiritus* is lost in Cosin's version; Dryden's 'Creator Spirit' preserves it.

This great hymn has for a thousand years been associated with many of the most solemn offices of the Church, at coronations, consecrations, and ordinations, for example. Its use at ordination services has not been traced earlier than the eleventh century, but its use at Pentecost can be traced to the tenth. Its importance was marked in medieval times by special ceremonies designed to invest the singing of it with greater dignity, the wearing of the best vestments, the use of incense, and the ringing of bells.

The anthem-form of Attwood's tune is given in *The Church Anthem Book*.

186 COME, THOU HOLY PARACLETE

This hymn, often in medieval times called the 'Golden Sequence', is not only one of the best examples of the sequence type of hymn, but 'one of the masterpieces of sacred Latin poetry'. Julian quotes the following appreciation of it from Clichtovaeus (1516): 'Nor indeed, in my opinion, can this piece be sufficiently praised; for it is above all praise, whether by reason of its wonderful sweetness along with a most clear and flowing style, or by reason of its agreeable brevity along with wealth and profusion of ideas, especially as every line expresses one idea, or finally by reason of the elegant grace of its structure, in which things contrasted are set over against each other, and most aptly linked together. And I well believe that the author (whoever he was), when he composed this piece, had his soul transfused by a certain heavenly sweetness, by which, the Holy Spirit being its author, he uttered so much sweetness in so few words.'

Of its authorship Mr. Gaselee says, in *The Oxford Book of Medieval Latin Verse*, that 'the ascriptions to King Robert II of France and Hermannus Contractus are certainly wrong: Pope Innocent III is a possibility, but the most probable author is Cardinal Stephen Langton, Archbishop of Canterbury.'

It is a striking witness to the extent to which this sequence had come into popular use throughout the Church, that when the immense multiplication of sequence hymns created one of the problems for which the Council of Trent had to find some redress, and the extreme measure was adopted, in 1570, of sweeping almost all of them out of permitted use, only five exceptions were made. Of these, this was one, the others being the *Dies Irae*, *Stabat Mater*, *Lauda Sion*, and *Victimae Paschali*; these alone remain in the Roman Missal to this day.

190 COME, HOLY SPIRIT, COME

Hart's hymn was written on Whit-Sunday, May 29, 1757. See Thomas Wright's *Life of Joseph Hart* (p. 42).

196 COME, HOLY GHOST, OUR HEARTS INSPIRE

ST. COLUMBA is No. 1043 in the Stanford-Petrie Collection.

205 THE CHURCH'S ONE FOUNDATION

Mr. Kendrick Pyne, long organist of the Cathedral and the Town Hall, Manchester, related in some published Memorials that he was a resident pupil in Wesley's house in Winchester when AURELIA was composed. The house had a large garden attached, which being very untidily kept, was known among the local musical wits as 'Wesley's *Wilderness*', this being also the name of one of his most famous anthems. One Sunday afternoon, Wesley was playing and improvising in his drawing-room alone, when suddenly and imperatively he summoned those members of his family who were within call, to listen to an idea that had occurred to him 'in the way of a popular tune'. He then played over the present tune, which subsequently received its name from the hymn for which it was written—'Urbs Sion aurea' (Jerusalem the Golden).

206 GLORIOUS THINGS OF THEE ARE SPOKEN

The tune is founded on a Croatian melody. In English collections it first appeared in Edward Miller's *Sacred Music* (1802). It is used in Germany as the tune of 'Deutschland über alles'.

212 FOR THE MIGHT OF THINE ARM WE BLESS THEE

Mrs. Hemans' 'Hymn of the Vaudois Mountain Christians' is inspired throughout by the thought of the mountains as the defence of God's people; e.g. the first verse:

> For the strength of the Hills we bless thee,
>   Our God, our Fathers' God;
> Thou hast made thy people mighty
>   By the touch of the mountain sod;
> Thou hast fixed our ark of refuge
>   Where the spoiler's feet ne'er trod:
> For the strength of the Hills we bless thee,
>   Our God, our Fathers' God.

215 THY HAND, O GOD, HAS GUIDED

THORNBURY was composed for the Twenty-fifth Annual Festival of the London Church Choir Association in 1898, and first appeared in the Association's Festival Book of Nov. 17, 1898; thereafter it was printed in the composer's *Hymn Tunes Original and Selected* (1905).

218 FOR THOSE WE LOVE WITHIN THE VEIL

Mr. Charter Piggott's hymn was written for a Commemoration Service early in the War (1915), in his church at Streatham. It was published in *Songs of Praise* (1925), and in *Congregational School Worship* (1926).

224 O WHAT THEIR JOY AND THEIR GLORY MUST BE

A fine translation of Abélard's *O quanta qualia*, by Miss Helen Waddell, will be found in *Medieval Latin Lyrics*. Unfortunately, she adopts a metre which does not suit the lovely proper tune.

> How mighty are the Sabbaths,
>   How mighty and how deep,
> That the high courts of heaven
>   To everlasting keep.
> What peace unto the weary,
>   What pride unto the strong,
> When God in Whom are all things
>   Shall be all things to men.

> Jerusalem is the city
> Of everlasting peace,
> A peace that is surpassing
> And utter blessedness;
> Where finds the dreamer waking
> Truth beyond dreaming far,
> Nor is the heart's possessing
> Less than the heart's desire. . . .

There is an anthem setting of this hymn in *The Church Anthem Book*.

225 HE WANTS NOT FRIENDS THAT HATH THY LOVE

The original form of KENT was as follows:

226 O BLEST

The peculiar metre of BRAINT, the first line consisting of two identical monosyllables, seems to have been derived from an old Welsh carol, 'Cloch, cloch,' or 'Tincian y cloch' ('Bell, Bell,' or 'Toll, Bell'). The words of this 'carol of praise and worship' are from *Bardd a Byrddau*, by Jonathan Hughes, 1788—a writer who in many other ballads and carols in this metre strictly adhered (as other writers have not always done) to the repeated monosyllabic word for the first line. See *The Welsh Folk-Song Journal*, vol. ii (1925), pp. 247–51.

The penultimate strain of this tune has been omitted by Ieuan Gwyllt and his successors. But in the unabridged Dorian form this strain, preceding the last four bars, to which the same words are repeated, runs thus:

The curious old form, mainly major, given below from the same *Journal*, is found, with negligible variations, in several old Welsh MS. tune-books. The editor noted it from an old precentor near

Portmadoc about forty years ago. Alternative names for BRAINT
are 'Trawsfynedd' and 'Union'.

227 LET SAINTS ON EARTH IN CONCERT SING

The first changes in Wesley's original (in five double verses) were
made in Cotterill's *Selection of Psalms and Hymns* (1815), possibly
by Montgomery, who was closely associated with Cotterill and contributed fifty hymns to his eighth edition; but the present version
appeared first in Murray's *Hymnal for Use in the English Church*
(1852), which is sometimes called Mosley's Hymnal, from the
name of the publisher. Murray (the Rev. Francis H. Murray of
Chislehurst) deserves particular remembrance as the originator of
the idea of *Hymns Ancient and Modern* and as one of the most
active members of the editorial committee that produced the first
edition of that epoch-making book. The version of this hymn
which he made is a masterpiece of editing. The first couplet is his
own; the second couplet of ver. 1 and vv. 2 and 3 are all Wesley's;
vv. 4 and 5 are Murray's superb emendation of the first quatrain
of Wesley's third and the second quatrain of Wesley's last verse.
Only at one point did Murray's fine sense fail him. Wesley wrote:

> 'Part of His host have cross'd the flood,
> And part are crossing now.'

The plural gives the idea of *multitude*—the 'militant, embodied
host'—much more finely than the singular, which is thin, and
also makes the lines too sibilant.

231 ALL LANDS AND PEOPLES, ALL THE EARTH

J. W. Elliott's tune, GLORIA IN EXCELSIS, was written in 1862 for
Trinity Sunday, and appeared in *Church Hymns with Tunes* (1st
ed., 1874) under the heading 'Choral Festival', to a hymn beginning:

> Hark! Hark! The organ loudly peals,
> Our thankful hearts inviting.

Elliott was practically the editor of *Church Hymns*, though Sullivan's name is on the title-page.

236 WE LOVE THE PLACE, O GOD

This hymn was written by William Bullock, then a young sailor-missionary, for the opening of a mission-chapel at Trinity Bay, Newfoundland, in 1827. Seventy years later a church replaced the chapel on the same site, and at its consecration, not only was this hymn in a revised form sung once more, but the sermon preached by its author at the opening of the chapel was read to the people.

242 BEHOLD US, LORD, A LITTLE SPACE

Canon Dearmer says of this hymn: 'It must be one of the earliest hymns in which science and art are mentioned and are recognized as part of God's work. . . . Free from the sentimentality of the period, it handles tersely and epigrammatically the modern world of business and labour, and after more than sixty years it is modern still.'

The history of the tune BEDFORD is fully discussed in the *Handbook* note on this hymn. Since the note was written, the undoubted matrix of the tune has been discovered by Miss Anne G. Gilchrist in the Proper Tune to the Hymn after Communion in Playford's Psalter of 1677. This tune, which is in three parts, Cantus, Medius, and Bassus, is as follows:

It looks as if Weale adapted this original; or it may be that both Playford and Weale adapted an earlier original in different ways. The similarity of the first line of the Playford tune to the third line of ROCKINGHAM (COMMUNION) will be noted.

244 O BE WITH US, GRACIOUS FATHER

DULCINA, with a second half different entirely from that in the MS. in the British Museum, is included in Forbes's *Cantus* to a carol, 'Of ye Birth of Christ', ver. 1 of which is as follows:

> Jurie cam to Jerussalem,
> All the warld was taxit then;
> Blissid Marie brought to Bethlem
> Moir than all the warld again:
> A gift so blist, so goode ye best
> That evir was sein, was hard or done,
> A King, a Chryst, prophet a priest,
> A Jesus God, a man a sone.

There is a setting of this carol by Sir Frederick Bridge.

246 DEAR SHEPHERD OF THY PEOPLE, HEAR
247 JESUS, WHERE'ER THY PEOPLE MEET

Newton found difficulty in attracting his people to the prayer meeting. One device he used to draw them was to provide a new hymn every Tuesday. In April, 1769, the meeting was moved 'to the great room in the Great House. It is a noble place', he wrote, 'with a parlour behind it, and holds 130 people conveniently.' It was to celebrate this move that these two hymns were written by Newton and Cowper respectively. This explains the reference in 'Thy former mercies here renew'. Another verse, now everywhere omitted, was the one quoted in the note on Hymn 247 in the *Handbook*; the last line of it should read, 'And bless us with a large increase.'

249 LIGHT OF THE ANXIOUS HEART

T. L. Hately, who was a member of R. A. Smith's choir in St. George's, Edinburgh, maintained that SELMA was of Smith's own composition. The tune, however, has considerable likeness to various airs sung to the folk-song 'I sowed the seeds of love', and probably is founded upon one of them heard traditionally by Smith. On the name, see note on MORVEN under Psalter Tunes.

250 ENTER THY COURTS, THOU WORD OF LIFE

The form of the FIFTH MODE MELODY which appears in *The Yattendon Hymnal* was discovered by Dr. Evans to be really the Faux Bourdon for the tune, and as such was set by him to ver. 2 in the *Hymnary*.

The tune itself appeared, under the name WATERBROOK, in 3/4 time, in *The Scottish Psalmody* (1854), set to Psalm xxv, 'Shew me Thy ways, O Lord', with the following note, highly characteristic of the time: 'This tasteful composition—taken from Dibdin's *Standard Tune Book*—is given as left by its distinguished author (Tallis), with the exception of a change from 2/4 to 3/4 time, in order to adapt it to congregational use.'

254 ALL THINGS ARE THINE; NO GIFT HAVE WE

HERR JESU CHRIST appeared in *Pensum Sacrum*, set to six of its
267 Latin odes, in the following form:

The tune takes its name from the hymn 'Herr Jesus Christ, dich zu uns wend', to which it was set in the *Gothäer Cantional* (1651).

261 CHRIST, WHOSE GLORY FILLS THE SKIES

In view of the fierce controversy between Toplady and the Wesleys it is of interest to note that Toplady included this hymn, without the author's name, in his *Psalms and Hymns* (1776). The belief grew up that he had written it, and was widely held until Montgomery disproved it, pointing out that the hymn was written in 1740, the year of Toplady's birth.

271 BEFORE THE DAY DRAWS NEAR ITS ENDING

Among the variants of the tune GOTTLOB, ES GEHT the last line of the form used in the published edition of Bach's *Choralgesänge* should be noted:

The original metre is 98.98.88.

274 AS NOW THE SUN'S DECLINING RAYS

There is an earlier ascription of BURFORD to Purcell than the one mentioned in the *Handbook* note—that made by Edward Miller in his *Psalms of David* (1790), where the tune is headed 'Said to be Purcell's'. See note on ST. THOMAS in the present Supplement (Psalter Tunes). Grove's *Dictionary of Music* still (1927 edition) definitely includes BURFORD among Purcell's works.

286 ABIDE WITH ME: FAST FALLS THE EVENTIDE

In the *Life of Frederick Denison Maurice*, by his son (vol. ii, p. 641), it is stated that this 'was always his favourite of all hymns: the one he was sure to select for any service that specially interested him.'

W. H. Monk's tune EVENTIDE is said to have been written in ten minutes. Judging from the frequency with which it is sung at popular gatherings such as international football matches, it is one of the best known of hymn-tunes, and has made 'Abide with me' the most popular of hymns.

288 NOW THE DAY IS OVER

The German tune which Baring-Gould heard as a child, and which, he came to believe, unconsciously suggested EUDOXIA to him, was in all probability that of a song which was very widely taught in schools about the middle of last century, *The Cricket*, by A. Weber. As noted by Miss Anne G. Gilchrist this tune is as follows:

Chirp-ing lit-tle crick-et, Chirp, and do not cease; . .

Sing-ing in the thick-et, Chirp a-way in peace. . .

Tra la la, tra la la, tra la la   la   la la la la la. . .   la. . .

Miss Gilchrist says: 'I think we may have here the German air of which EUDOXIA is a "reminiscence"—though it does not seem to be more. The metre of Baring-Gould's verses is the same, and I think there may have been in his mind a sub-conscious association of ideas with a hazy remembrance of tune and words heard as a child, and giving an impression of night-time and peace:

> While the world is sleeping
> Chirp away in peace—

so forming the germ both of verses and tune. But a "reminiscence" is a long way from being an adaptation, and I think Baring-Gould had a right to call the tune he made for his hymn his own.'

There is, however, a children's evening hymn, No. 1356 in the *Plymouth Collection* (1856), set to this German tune, without the refrain, and very much of the same character as Baring-Gould's. It begins:

> See, the light is fading
> From the western sky;
> Day, thou art departing,
> Night is drawing nigh.

Is this an intermediate link?

289 THE DAY THOU GAVEST, LORD, IS ENDED

The proper rhythm of LES COMMANDEMENS DE DIEU, as Bourgeois wrote it, is as follows:

291 ALL PRAISE TO THEE, MY GOD, THIS NIGHT

'This is a perfect canon, in that the necessities of the form nowhere obtrude themselves, the tune being as clear and "natural" as if these necessities did not exist' (*Songs of Praise Discussed*). In the original, the tenors led, the sopranos followed, when the tune was sung in canon form, as in the full version in the *Hymnary*. Tallis was fond of this device. In his monkish days he and his fellow inmates of the cloisters used to amuse themselves in this way. To *The Black Sanctus or Monks' Hymn to Saint Satan* he set a canon in three parts, and King Henry VIII, musical enthusiast as he was, would sometimes delight in taking part.

292 SUN OF MY SOUL, THOU SAVIOUR DEAR

The significance of the opening of this famous hymn is not evident unless the first two verses of the poem are quoted, as they deserve to be, for their own beauty, as well as to furnish the background of the poet's thought. The sun has gone down, and the traveller must pursue his way without its light; but the Sun of the soul will never set.

> 'Tis gone, that bright and orbéd blaze,
> Fast fading from our wistful gaze;
> Yon mantling cloud has hid from sight
> The last faint pulse of quivering light.
>
> In darkness and in weariness
> The traveller on his way must press,
> No gleam to watch on tree or tower
> Whiling away the lonesome hour.
>
> Sun of my soul, Thou Saviour dear,
> It is not night if Thou be near. . . .

It is a tradition that it was in the rectory garden at East Leach that Keble wrote this hymn. In an article in *The Church Quarterly Review*, vol. cv, the Rev. Canon E. F. Smith, vicar of Tewkesbury, says: 'Certainly the first two verses (generally omitted when it is sung as a hymn) would fit in well with the westward aspect looking from that garden westward towards Fairford across the dark woods and winding ways.' Referring to the description of the benighted traveller in the second verse, he goes on to say: 'Such was in fact the unpleasant experience of Isaac Williams when he first went as a pupil to John Keble, and walked over from Southrop to find Dean Farm, where he lodged: it was evening when he set out with Hurrell Froude, and a thick mist came on: the night grew perfectly dark, and they wandered about (Williams tells us) the whole night till near the morning.'

The date of the Irish *Church Hymnal* in which ABENDS first appeared should be 1873.

HERR GOTT VATER is set in *Tisch Gesänge* (Breslau, 1615) to a Grace before Meat, beginning:

> Herr Gott, Vater im Himmelreich,
> Wir, deine kinder allzugleich,
> Bitten dich jetzt aus Herzensgrund:
> Speise uns auch zu dieser Stund.

This tune would perfectly suit the Grace before Meat (Hymn 656), 'Be present at our table, Lord'.

293 GOD, THAT MADEST EARTH AND HEAVEN

Heber's evening hymn of one verse was written to the Welsh air *Ar hyd y nos* (All through the night), played by a Welsh harper in the hall of a house where he was a visitor—either at Llangedwyn, near Oswestry, where he often stayed with the Hon. C. W. W. Wynn, or at Bodryddan, near Rhuddlan, the house of his father-in-law, Dean Shipley. It is set to this Welsh air in the choir-book arranged by his sister Mary (afterwards Mrs. Cholmondeley) before 1822, for use at Hodnet Church.

294 ERE I SLEEP, FOR EVERY FAVOUR

THANET first appeared in Jowett's *Musæ Solitariæ* (1823).

297 COME, DEAREST LORD, DESCEND AND DWELL

Lawes's tunes have not the attractiveness of those which Gibbons wrote for Wither's verses. His music was characterized by Hawkins (according to Dr. Johnson 'a very unclubable man') as deficient in melody and as being 'neither recitative nor air, but in so precise a medium between both that a name is wanting for it'. According to Sir Henry Hadow, however, 'it was not Lawes's object to produce melody in the proper sense of the word, but to set "words with just note and accent", to make the prosody of his text his principal care; and it was doubtless that quality which induced all the best poetical writers of his day, from Milton and Waller downwards, to desire that their verses should be set by him.' Milton's sonnet 'To Mr. H. Lawes on his Airs', from which Sir Henry quotes, has these lines:

> Harry, whose tuneful and well-measured song
>   First taught our English Music how to span
>   Words with just note and accent, not to scan
> With Midas' ears, committing short and long,
> Thy worth and skill exempts thee from the throng,
>   With praise enough for Envy to look wan;
>   To after age thou shalt be writ the man
> That with smooth air couldst humour best our tongue.
> Thou honour'st Verse, and Verse must lend her wing
>   To honour thee, the priest of Phoebus' quire,
>   That tunest their happiest lines in hymn or story.

299 LORD, DISMISS US WITH THY BLESSING

The omitted third stanza illustrates the change of thought that has taken place in hymnody since the hymn was written 150 years ago:

> So whene'er the Signal's given
> Us from Earth to call away,
> Borne on Angels' wings to Heaven,
> Glad the Summons to obey,
> May we ever
> Reign with Christ in endless Day.

309 BY COOL SILOAM'S SHADY RILL

The first two lines of this hymn have been caustically described, by one who has intimate knowledge of the conditions in present-day Jerusalem, as containing 'the maximum of mis-statement in the minimum of space'.

310 GRACIOUS SAVIOUR, GENTLE SHEPHERD

BRYNTIRION is in *Chants Chrétiens* set to Cantique 110, which begins thus:

> O Jésus, dans ta bergerie
> Introduis tes heureux troupeaux;
> Garde ton Église chérie,
> Et nous pais comme tes agneaux.
> Que tous les enfants de lumière
> Remplis de ton Esprit d'amour
> S'entr'aiment partout sur la terre
> Jusqu'au moment de ton retour.

313 ACCORDING TO THY GRACIOUS WORD

Burns's reference to BANGOR in *The Ordination* should be quoted, as illustrating both the popularity of the tune in his time, and the quality of the singing:

> Mak' haste an' turn King David owre,
> An' lilt wi' holy clangor;
> O' double verse come gie us four,
> An' skirl up the 'Bangor'.

Barthélémon's song, referred to in the *Handbook* note, seems to have travelled out to America described as 'a pathetic Scotch ballad'! There the melody became a hymn-tune, preserving its original form, save for the smoothing out of one or two dotted notes, &c. As an '8s and 7s Double' it occurs in several American hymn-books of the 'sixties under the name of AUTUMN or BETHLEHEM, and is described as 'Spanish', from a mistaken idea that the tune as well as the words of Monk Lewis's song was taken from the

Spanish. In Dadmun's *Melodeon*, 1861, it is set to 'Glorious things of thee are spoken' as follows:

The original song begins:

> Sad and fearful is the story
> Of the Roncesvales fight,
> On those fatal plains of glory
> Perished many a gallant knight.

Durandarte, a brave knight, was slain by the Moors at Roncesvalles in Spain. Belerma was his beloved lady.

317 AUTHOR OF LIFE DIVINE

It is a curious fact that this hymn never appeared in any of the official hymn-books of Methodism from 1780 until the most recent *Methodist Hymn Book* appeared in 1933. It came into common use through its publication in the 1875 revised edition of *Hymns Ancient and Modern*.

With the opening strain of AUCTOR VITAE cf. the Pilgrim's Song in *Parsifal*.

318 BREAD OF THE WORLD, IN MERCY BROKEN

The musical editor of *Songs of Praise Discussed* says of PSALM CXVIII (RENDEZ À DIEU): 'This lovely and impressive tune is in some ways the finest of all the early psalm-tunes; it is perfectly proportioned; it begins with a phrase of remarkable expressiveness, and continues with others as significant as they are logically consistent, while the beauty of the change of rhythm in the downward scale of the fifth line is extraordinary. This is a tune which gives the true "spinal thrill"; of its kind it is unsurpassed.' All this is justly said of one of the loveliest church tunes ever written.

319 THEE WE ADORE, O HIDDEN SAVIOUR, THEE

The lines of the original in which 'Pious Pelican' occurs are as follows:

> Pie pellicane Jesu Domine,
> Me immundum munda tuo sanguine.

320 AND NOW, O FATHER, MINDFUL OF THE LOVE

In a note on this hymn, in *Songs of Praise Discussed*, the use of the words 'And now' at the beginning is criticized, and attention called to the number of hymns 'disfigured by this unnecessary commencement'. Blake is excused for beginning 'Jerusalem' with the words 'And did those feet', on the ground that that poem occurs after two paragraphs as part of the preface to his *Milton*. But a preface to Bright's hymn has to be understood. The clue to what was in his mind is given by W. H. Monk in the title he gave the tune. UNDE ET MEMORES are the opening words of the prayer in the Roman canon of the Mass which occurs after the consecration of the elements, at the elevation of the chalice: 'Unde et memores, Domine, nos servi tui sed et plebs tua sancta', &c.: 'Wherefore, O Lord, we, Thy servants, as also Thy holy people, remembering the blessed passion of the same Christ Thy Son our Lord,' &c. Bright assumes that those who sing the hymn will set it mentally in the context of all that has led up to the moment preceding participation; the 'And now' is the fitting opening for what is intended as the *aditus* to the consummating act.

324 DECK THYSELF, MY SOUL, WITH GLADNESS

Schumann wrote thus to Mendelssohn after hearing him play Bach's organ setting of SCHMÜCKE DICH—one of the most beautiful of Bach's organ chorales: 'Round the *cantus firmus* hung golden garlands of leaves, and such blissfulness was breathed from within it, that you yourself avowed that if life was bereft of all hope and faith, this one chorale could renew them for you. I was silent and went away dazed into God's acre, feeling acutely pained that I could lay no flower on his urn.' (*Musik und Musiker*, vol. i, p. 153.)

333 POUR OUT THY SPIRIT FROM ON HIGH

This hymn appeared in the year in which it was written, 1833, for J. Birchell's *Selection of Hymns*, and in the same year in Edward Bickersteth's *Christian Psalmody*.

337 LORD OF LIGHT, WHOSE NAME OUTSHINETH

The Welsh song from which LLANSANNAN is derived is 'Y Gwelltyn Glas' (The green blade). See *Journal of the Welsh Folk-Song Society*, vol. ii, p. 79.

347 HERE, LORD, WE OFFER THEE ALL THAT IS FAIREST

For a description of St. Luke's, Chelsea, for which this hymn was written, see Henry Kingsley's *The Hillyars and the Burtons*, ch. 23.

BLODYN means not 'flowers' but 'a flower'; the plural is *blodau*.

349 FATHER, WHO ON MAN DOST SHOWER

The carol QUEM PASTORES LAUDAVERE appears with the original words in *The Oxford Book of Carols* (1928). It was much used at Christmastide during the ceremonies round the crib in churches. Its widespread use is evident from the number of collections, both Roman and Protestant in which it appears, from 1555, when it was first published in F. Triller's *Ein Schlesich singebüchlein aus Göttlicher schrifft*, &c. (Breslau), downwards. In the usual form of the melody the last bar of the first three lines is syncopated thus:

353 FATHER, WHOSE WILL IS LIFE AND GOOD

TALLIS is often called TALLIS'S ORDINAL because in Archbishop Parker's *The Whole Psalter translated into English Metre* (vide *Handbook* note on Hymn 250), in which it first appeared, it was set to the version of *Veni, Creator Spiritus* used in the Prayer Book Ordination service. Of the nine tunes written by Tallis for this Psalter, eight were in the eight ecclesiastical modes; the present one follows them. This instruction was printed with them: 'The tenor of these partes be for the people when they will synge alone; the other parts, put for greater queers, or such as will syng or play them privatlye.' The present tune differs from the others, however, in that it has the melody in the top part and not in the tenor.

355 O LORD OF LIFE, AND LOVE, AND POWER

The fact that this hymn was written for the opening of a new Sunday School is evident in an omitted verse, between 2 and 3:

> In this new house our hands have raised
> Thy service to pursue,
> O may Thy name henceforth be praised
> By work more pure and true.
> May child and teacher evermore
> Come here with earnest heart,
> And those who never worked before
> Stand forth and bear their part.

371 FROM GREENLAND'S ICY MOUNTAINS

The air for which Heber wrote the hymn was, ''Twas when the sea was roaring'. Mason's tune was written at the request of a lady who had just received the hymn from a friend in England; thereafter it was published as indicated in the *Handbook*.

373 FAR ROUND THE WORLD THY CHILDREN SING THEIR SONG

The hymn was written in 1909 for a Sunday School Anniversary at Bowes Park, London; the verses on Asia, Africa, and the Islands were added three years later.

374 ONCE AGAIN, DEAR LORD, WE PRAY

MORNING, No. 3, in *The European Psalmist*, was originally in 3/2 time, and was set to 'Wake and lift up thyself, my heart' (Hymn 256).

389 HARK! THE SONG OF JUBILEE

The original broadsheet on which this hymn was printed says that it was 'composed at the express desire of the London Missionary Society, with a special reference to the renunciation of Idolatry and acknowledgement of the Gospel, in the Georgian Isles of the South Seas', and sung at Spa Fields Chapel, London, May 14, 1818.

403 LORD JESUS, THINK ON ME

The extent of the liberty Chatfield allowed himself in making this 'paraphrase or amplification' of Synesius' original, is shown in the following literal prose translation of the Greek poem, made by Dr. Costley White, Head Master of Westminster School:

> Be mindful, Christ, Son of God,
> Who rulest on high, of thy servant,
> Sinful of heart, who wrote these words.
> And grant to me release from passions breeding death,
> Which are inborn in my unclean soul.
> But give me to behold, Saviour Jesus,
> Thy divine brightness, wherein appearing
> > I shall sing a song
> > To the healer of souls,
> > To the healer of limbs,
> > With the great Father
> > > And the Holy Spirit.

ST. BRIDE was originally called 'St. Bridget's' after Wren's well-known church (St. Bride's) off Fleet Street, where Dr. Howard was organist. Later, it was known simply as 'Bridget's'.

405 LORD, IN THIS THY MERCY'S DAY

HEILIGER GEIST appeared eight years before the date first indicated in the *Handbook*—1639—in D. G. Corner's *Gross Catolisch Gesangbuch* (1631), and also, later, in the same editor's *Geistliche Nachtigall der Catholischen Teütschen*, &c. (Vienna, 1648).

411 JUST AS I AM, WITHOUT ONE PLEA

Bishop Moule of Durham, a relative of Charlotte Elliott, stated that the origin of this hymn was, that at a time when the authoress's brother, the Rev. Henry Venn Elliott, of Brighton, was holding a bazaar in St. Mary's Hall there, to raise funds for the building of a school, Charlotte lay awake all night, oppressed with the feeling of uselessness and 'tossed about with many a doubt'. While every one else was out and busy with the bazaar on the following day, she lay at home, in greater misery than ever; and it was in her effort to fight her depression off that she took her pen and wrote the hymn.

After her death over a thousand letters thanking her for this hymn were found.

413 ROCK OF AGES, CLEFT FOR ME

The hymn was first published in *The Gospel Magazine*, March, 1776. Where did Toplady get his inspiration? The following passage from Dr. Brevint's *The Christian Sacrament and Sacrifice*, prefixed to John and Charles Wesley's *Hymns of the Lord's Supper* (1745), seems to give the answer: 'O Rock of Israel, Rock of Salvation, Rock struck and cleft for me, let those two streams of blood and water which once gushed out of Thy side bring down pardon and holiness into my soul; and let me thirst after them now, as if I stood upon the mountain whence sprung this water, and near the cleft of that rock, the wounds of my Lord, whence gushed this sacred blood.' This, and the current use of 'Rock of Ages' as a name for Christ in and before Toplady's day, furnish a much more probable explanation of the origin of the hymn than the widely credited legend connected with Burrington Combe in the Mendips. (See note on the hymn in the *Handbook*.)

No such originative suggestion, however, detracts from the pure inspiration of the hymn. Canon Dearmer thus expresses his reluctant admiration: 'There may be here some influence of early associations, to which we are all subject; but the intensity of religious passion has surely endued Toplady with a power beyond his normal gifts: there is such vigour of unconscious art—the violence of the opening cry, the sweeping negatives of the second and third verses, the growing exultation of the last, and the quiet return at the end, in a changed tone of gentle confidence, to the opening words. It may be questioned whether we ought to sing the hymn to-day; but it remains a notable monument of the religion which gripped our fathers.'—*Songs of Praise Discussed*, p. 337.

NICHT SO TRAURIG is from Freylinghausen's *Neues Geistreiches Gesangbuch* (1714), where it is set to Gerhardt's 'Nicht so traurig, nicht so sehr'.

414 JESUS, LOVER OF MY SOUL

This was Henry Ward Beecher's favourite hymn. He said of it: 'I would rather have written that hymn than have the fame of all the kings that ever sat on earth; it has more power in it.'

'The nearer waters roll' is borrowed from Prior, of whom the Wesleys thought highly.

HOLLINGSIDE, though not published till 1861, was probably written during Dykes's time of residence in Hollingside Cottage, 1850–3. (See *Musical Times*, October 1904.) The reharmonization of the tune has lost a neat bit of imitation in the fifth line.

ABERYSTWYTH was so named because Joseph Parry, when he composed it, was Professor of Music in University College in that town.

416 COME, O THOU TRAVELLER UNKNOWN

C. E. Vulliamy, referring to John Wesley's emotion when he gave out this hymn a fortnight after Charles's death, says: 'For the first time in a ministry of fifty years he broke down in public under the stress of a personal emotion.'

417 HARK, MY SOUL! IT IS THE LORD

NUN KOMM, DER HEIDEN HEILAND is a simplified form of the plainsong melody associated with the hymn 'Veni Redemptor Gentium'. It is found in the Erfurt *Enchiridion* of 1524 as well as in Walther's Wittenberg *Gesangbuchlein* of the same year; it occurs also in other books of that time.

420 JESUS, THOU JOY OF LOVING HEARTS
421 JESUS! THE VERY THOUGHT IS SWEET
422 JESUS, THE VERY THOUGHT OF THEE
423 O JESUS, KING MOST WONDERFUL

The *Handbook* note on these centos from 'Jesu, dulcis memoria' is in error, owing to a misunderstanding of Dom Pothier's words in the *Revue du Chant Grégorien*. These words in turn are shown by Reginald Vaux in *The Church Quarterly Review* of April, 1929, to have rested on a misquotation of Dom Guéranger's *L'Année Liturgique*. That again was based on an otherwise unsupported statement of Mabillon, who edited Bernard's works in the early eighteenth century. To make confusion worse confounded, so high an authority as Bishop W. H. Frere, in his invaluable Notes in the Historical Edition of *Hymns Ancient and Modern*, p. 357, states that Dom Pothier 'has found the hymn in MSS. of the eleventh century, ascribed to a Benedictine Abbess'. Of this discovery no trace can be found in Dom Pothier's own words.

The pungent language of Mr. Vaux on all this is thus fully justified: 'Upon the narrow and insecure foundation laid down by Mabillon . . . subsequent commentators have raised a structure that it will not support: by a seeming corroboration of his statement that is in fact probably nothing more than repetition: by additions thereto based upon inference: and even by unintentional errors that have become canonized through the eminence of the writers they have deceived, and by whom they have been quoted in good faith.'

Dogmatic statements like this—'It is not by St. Bernard. . . . While a few verses were added later, the poem itself has been found in a manuscript of the eleventh century' (*Songs of Praise Discussed*), are quite unwarranted by the facts. The one thing certain is that the picturesque figure of the eleventh century Benedictine Abbess, the supposed supplanter of St. Bernard in the authorship of the hymn, has vanished into thin air.

So good an authority as Archbishop Trench believed the attribution of the hymn to St. Bernard to be well founded. Of all the hymns so ascribed, with one exception, he said: 'If he did not write, it is not easy to guess who could have written them; and indeed they bear profoundly the stamp of his mind, being only inferior in beauty to his prose.' Dr. G. G. Coulton takes an opposite view. Bernard, he says, 'disapproved of poetry, and indeed it was one of the clauses of the *Carta Caritatis* that no Cistercian should compose verse. When Bernard wrote the Office for St. Victor's Day at the request of the Victorines of Paris, the hymns were purposely composed so that they would not scan, though they lent themselves to chanting.' (*Five Centuries of Religion*, vol. i, p. 301.) Mr. Stephen Gaselee, in *The Oxford Book of Medieval Latin Verse*, ventures upon a new suggestion, that, judging from the nationality of the best MSS. of the poem, the author may possibly be of English origin. Certainty is impossible, and in the absence of positive evidence for any theory, all that can be said is that the hymn is 'attributed to St. Bernard', and that it was ascribed to him within about a century of his death.

422 JESUS, THE VERY THOUGHT OF THEE

ROCHESTER was issued separately in sheet form by Curwen in 1924, Hylton Stewart being then organist of Rochester Cathedral. It was included in *Songs of Praise* in the following year.

424 O LOVE THAT WILT NOT LET ME GO·

It was in January 1882 that the hymn appeared in *Life and Work*. In 1885 it appeared in *The Scottish Hymnal*. Dr. Matheson's memory must therefore have been at fault when he said that the hymn was composed at Innellan in June 1882, six months after its publication. Probably the year was 1881.

428 O LOVE DIVINE, HOW SWEET THOU ART

The tune ALLGÜTIGER, MEIN PREISGESANG in its original form gives the fifth line, not as a reproduction of the fourth, but thus:

432 JESUS, THY BOUNDLESS LOVE TO ME

In the *Handbook* note on this hymn 'the Mark of Brandenburg' should be 'the Westphalian county of Mark'.

434 LOVED WITH EVERLASTING LOVE

For the thought of ver. 2 cf. Henry Martyn's *Cambridge Diary*: 'Since I have known God in a saving manner, painting, poetry, and music have had charms unknown to me before; for Religion has refined my mind, and made it susceptible of impressions from the sublime and beautiful.'

436 IT IS A THING MOST WONDERFUL

SOLOTHURN is used by Beethoven as the theme for his *Variationen über ein Schweizerlied*. 'The tune, both in rhythm and general form, has several counterparts among Swiss folk songs, and, in particular, resembles strongly "Dursli und Bäbeli", which may be found in *Sammlung von Schweizer Kühreihen und Volksliedern* (1826), a large collection of such songs, while others may be found in *Lieder aus der Schweiz*, &c. (1837) and *Recueil de Chants populaires suisses* (1920). Apart from the *ranz-des-vaches*, which is of necessity formed on the harmonies of the Alpine horn, the Swiss folk-tunes are mostly of a very simple type, though often attractively gay and rhythmic; the present tune is a good specimen of a more staid kind.' (*Songs of Praise Discussed.*)

438 THE KING OF LOVE MY SHEPHERD IS

Dr. Dykes died on Jan. 22, 1876. 'He was laid to rest at St. Oswald's, Durham, amid a vast concourse of friends, to the strains of this hymn.'

DUNAHA is a small village in County Clare, near the mouth of the Shannon, where John Hore, the blacksmith-poet, was born (*floruit c.* 1780).

The hymn to which he set the tune is a song of penitence written towards the end of his life, and first published in O'Daly's *Irish Miscellany* (1876). The original name of the tune is *Muinntear na n-Déis* (People of the Decies—a tract in Co. Waterford).

446 MY HEART IS RESTING, O MY GOD

The name of the tune PENTATONE is explained by the fact that it is in the 'Caledonian' five-note scale.

454 O GOD, THOU ART THE FATHER

See note on Hymn 179.

The Limerick sea-song 'Captain Thomson' is No. 380 in Joyce.

455 O HELP US, LORD; EACH HOUR OF NEED

In many hymn-books vv. 4 and 5 are omitted, following the example of Dean Milman in his *Selection of Psalms and Hymns*

45

(1837), so that the remaining verses should all begin with 'O help us, Lord'. For certain uses, however, the loss of these verses weakens the hymn.

457 O FOR A CLOSER WALK WITH GOD

Strange myths have gathered round MARTYRDOM, one asserting that it is 'partly borrowed from a Covenanting melody', and another even that it was written by David Rizzio! Much more likely is the theory that it had a ballad origin. R. A. Smith described it as an 'Old Scottish Melody', and though in the lawsuit which arose upon his publication of it evidence enough was produced to show that Wilson had composed it, the possibility remained that it was suggested to Wilson's mind by a traditional tune. In *The Choir* for July, 1934, Miss Anne G. Gilchrist traces affinities between it and versions of the air of 'Helen of Kirkconnel', and affirms her belief that Smith was right in recognizing the tune as a traditional melody. Wilson was dead before Smith published the tune with the attribution of it to a traditional source; it is impossible, therefore, not to wonder whether, if he had been alive when Smith's claim was made, he would not have confirmed it. The lawsuit was concerned only with the publisher's property right. Whatever its origin, the comment on the tune in *Songs of Praise Discussed* will meet with agreement: 'The tune was certainly worth a dispute, for it would have been a credit to any composer; on the other hand, if, as it seems, R. A. Smith was responsible for re-writing it in triple time, a large part of the credit must be his, since the beauty of the melody is immensely enhanced by the change.'

463 MY SOUL, THERE IS A COUNTRY

In *The Oxford Book of Carols* (1928) there is this note on the tune CHERRY-TREE CAROL: 'The whole story of carol-music is summed up in an incident related by Baring-Gould: about 1865 he was teaching carols to mill-girls in the West Riding; and amongst them that by Dr. Gauntlett—"St. Joseph was a walking"—when they burst out with "Nay! we know one a great deal better nor yond", and lifting up their voices, they sang'—the Cherry-Tree Carol. Though it is taken from Husk's *Songs of the Nativity* (1868), therefore it had been traditional long before that; it was printed on broadsides in all parts of England.

Sandys, an early collector, barred the tune wrongly, so that it cannot be sung as he noted it, and it is doubtful whether Husk's interpretation, here followed, as in *The Oxford Book of Carols*, is what Sandys really intended. Cecil Sharp noted (also in Cornwall) a variant of the same air in triple time, and by altering the barring, Sandys's tune falls into the same measure—the usual one for Cherry-Tree Carol tunes. See *Folk-Song Journal*, vol. v, pp. 11–14.

464 MAKE ME A CAPTIVE, LORD

LEOMINSTER was composed for Dr. Bonar's 'A few more years shall roll'. Martin's own name for it was 'The Pilgrim Song'. Sir Arthur Sullivan, in *Church Hymns*, wrote a new harmony for the tune, and made slight changes in rhythm and melody, e.g. at the end of lines 2 and 4 ♩. ♩ ♩, and in line 7:

469 JESUS, FROM THY THRONE ON HIGH

LEBBAEUS appeared without any composer's name in *The St. Albans Tune Book* (1863).

471 O THOU WHO CAMEST FROM ABOVE

This hymn is taken by the Rev. F. Luke Wiseman, in his *Charles Wesley, Evangelist and Poet*, as an illustration of how scriptural language and thought is the warp and woof of the texture of Wesley's poetry. It is based on the passage in Lev. vi. 13, 'Fire shall be kept burning upon the altar continually; it shall not go out.' But in expatiating on the passage, line after line is indebted to some scriptural passage for its expression:

> O Thou who camest from above,[1]
> The pure celestial[3] fire[2] to impart,
> Kindle[2] a flame[4] of sacred love
> On the mean altar[5] of my heart.
> There let it for Thy glory[6] burn
> With inextinguishable[7] blaze,
> And trembling[8] to its source return
> In humble prayer[9] and fervent praise.
> Jesus, confirm my heart's desire[10]
> To work, and speak, and think for Thee;
> Still let me guard[11] the holy fire,
> And still stir up[12] Thy gift in me.
> Ready[13] for all Thy perfect will,[14]
> My acts of[15] faith and love repeat,
> Till death Thy endless mercies seal,[16]
> And make the sacrifice[17] complete.

[1] John iii. 31.
[2] Luke xii. 49; 2 Chron. vii. 3.
[3] 1 Kings xviii. 38; 1 Cor. xv. 40.
[4] Isaiah xliii. 2.
[5] Lev. ix. 24; Chron. xxi. 26.
[6] 2 Cor. iv. 15; viii. 19.
[7] Lev. vi. 13.
[8] Job v. 7, margin.
[9] James iv. 6–10.
[10] Rom. x. 1.
[11] Lev. vi. 13.
[12] 2 Tim. i. 6 (Greek).
[13] Titus iii. 1.
[14] Rom. xii. 2.
[15] 1 Thess. i. 3.
[16] Ephes. iv. 30.
[17] Phil. ii. 17; 2 Tim. iv. 6; Heb. xiii. 15–16.

472 FOR THEE, MY GOD, FOR THEE ALONE

BRISTOL appeared in Vincent Novello's *The Psalmist* (Part iv, 1842), but was not written for it; Wesley died in 1839.

478 BLEST ARE THE PURE IN HEART

This, on the Purification, was the earliest written of all the poems in *The Christian Year*, the first in the MS. of 1820. An anthem setting of this hymn, by Sir Walford Davies, is in *The Church Anthem Book*.

479 LOVE DIVINE, ALL LOVES EXCELLING

The Rev. F. Luke Wiseman, in his *Charles Wesley, Evangelist and Poet*, has this interesting note on this hymn: 'Without doubt his muse was set going by the "Song of Venus" from Dryden's play, *King Arthur*. Probably, however, it was not the words but Purcell's entrancing aria to which they were set which haunted his ear. At any rate, the hymn was sung to this melody. At one and the same time, therefore, our Sir Galahad rescued this captive melody from Dryden's amorous words, and the great word "Love" from its bondage to the heathen goddess, united the two, and set them free for the glorious service of their heavenly Lord. So Dryden's words,

> Fairest Isle, all Isles Excelling,
>   Seat of Pleasures, and of Loves;
> Venus here will chuse her Dwelling,
>   And forsake her *Cyprian* Groves.
>
> Cupid, from his Fav'rite Nation
>   Care and Envy will Remove;
> Jealousy that poysons Passion
>   And Despair that dies for Love,

are transfigured into

> Love Divine, all loves excelling, &c.'

A verse in the original of the hymn was omitted in *The Wesleyan Hymn Book* of 1780, and has been generally omitted since, to the great gain of the hymn:

> Breathe, O breathe Thy living Spirit
>   Into every troubled Breast,
> Let us all in Thee inherit,
>   Let us find that Second Rest.
> Take away our power of sinning,
>   Alpha and Omega be;
> End of Faith as its beginning,
>   Set our hearts at liberty.

The aria of Purcell referred to as inspiring the hymn appeared in *Sacred Harmony* under the name WESTMINSTER, as follows:

Love di - vine, all loves... ex - cell - ing,
Fix in us thy hum - ble dwell - ing,

Joy ... of heav'n .. to earth come down;
All ... thy faith - - ful mer - cies crown;

Je - - su, thou .. art all ... com - pas - sion,

Pure .. un - bound - ed love thou art;

Vis - it us with thy .. sal - va - tion,

En - ter ev - - 'ry trem - bling heart.

481 FATHER OF PEACE, AND GOD OF LOVE

It is interesting to note how the name—Andrew Tait—of the putative composer of ST. PAUL misled Henry Edward Dibdin, who had evidently only heard, not seen it, into a wild guess at his identity; in *The Standard Psalm Tune Book* (1850) he ascribed the tune to Nahum Tate! By the time his historical preface to the book was written, however, he had discovered that he was mistaken, for he wrote there as follows: 'This tune is not clearly traced. These are the facts connected with it. 1st.—It is not in Tate's Supplement, 1703. 2nd.—It is in William Gray's Collection of Psalm Tunes, Edinburgh, 1758. Dr. Mainzer assigns the tune to William Tate. If he had sufficient authority for so doing, the question is settled so far as Nahum Tate is concerned. It is probably of Scottish origin.'

The title of Chalmers's book, which Tait is believed to have edited, as given in the third edition, was: *A New and Correct Set of Church Tunes*, viz. [twenty-three tunes named] *with the Scale and Directions. Dedicated to the Provost, Baillies, and Permanent Members of Town Council, 'Encouragers and Promoters of useful Learning'.*

491 ALMIGHTY FATHER, WHO DOST GIVE

Bishop Masterman's hymn first appeared in *In Hoc Signo* (1916).

493 FATHER OF MEN, IN WHOM ARE ONE

Shuttleworth, a follower of Maurice and Kingsley in their Christian Socialism, wrote this hymn for the members of a club in connexion with his church of St. Nicholas Cole Abbey. It appeared in 1897 in the *Hymnal Appendix* (to *Church Hymns*) issued for use in that church, and, with music by the author, in his *Church Monthly* in the following year.

495 SAVIOUR, WHILE MY HEART IS TENDER

The ballad referred to, from which SHIPSTON is derived, is to be found in *English County Songs*, p. 71.

497 JUST AS I AM, THINE OWN TO BE

SAFFRON WALDEN was written for Charlotte Elliott's hymn 'O holy Saviour, Friend unseen'.

498 LORD, IN THE FULNESS OF MY MIGHT

The contemporary Cambridge tune-book referred to in the *Handbook* note on UNIVERSITY was Pieter Hellendaal's *A Collection of Psalms for the use of Parish Churches*, &c. (Cambridge, 1780). The fact that Randall was a contributor to this book, and that in his own *Collection of Psalm Tunes* (1754) he made no claim to the tune, makes it extremely unlikely that he was the composer.

501 'TAKE UP THY CROSS,' THE SAVIOUR SAID

The date given for *As Hymnodus Sacer* in the *Handbook* note— 1652—is a misprint for 1625. BRESLAU is a recast of the folk-song 'Ich fahr dahin', from the *Locheimer Liederbuch*, *c.* 1452.

504 THINE FOR EVER! GOD OF LOVE

The year of Archbishop Benson's death was 1896.

Wesley's name for the tune here named SAVANNAH was HERRNHUT, his SAVANNAH being quite a different tune.

506 I BIND UNTO MYSELF TO-DAY

ST. PATRICK is tune No. 1048 in the complete Petrie collection.

517 FIGHT THE GOOD FIGHT

The tune PENTECOST is altered to common time in the *Students' Hymnal*. This alteration is stated to have been made with the consent of the composer, who had been grieved at the alienation of his tune from its *Veni Creator* association by its annexation to a hymn of so different a character. Since it is now so firmly welded to the present hymn, the editor of the *Students' Hymnal* evidently judged that the best thing to be done was to suit it better to these words by setting it to a more vigorous rhythm, suggesting a march-tune rather than a devotional hymn, thus:

520 WORKMAN OF GOD! O LOSE NOT HEART

It is fair to say that the tradition that MARTYRS was sung by the Covenanters at Drumclog as they marched into battle probably originated with Sir Walter Scott. There is no trustworthy anterior evidence for it. The Laird of Torfoot's *Narrative of Drumclog and Bothwell Bridge* says that the aged men who stayed behind sang a cheering psalm to the tune MARTYRS, but does not say what psalm it was; then says that the fighting men, as they were in order opposite to Claverhouse and ready to join battle, sang a part of Psalm lxxvi, but makes no mention of the tune to which they sang it. The authenticity of this *Narrative*, however, is open to the gravest doubt.

There was no conventicle at Drumclog. One had been in process at Loudoun Hill, but broke up when word came that Claverhouse was on the march. The Covenanters then moved to meet him in a better strategic position. Claverhouse in his account of the engagement says plainly that they had sent away their women and children, and that when he saw them he found that they were 'drawn up in battle, upon a most advantageous ground, to which there was no coming but through mosses and lakes'. This last detail is fairly conclusive evidence against the tradition.

The late Rev. James Mearns, of *The Dictionary of Hymnology*, an expert assayer of the value of evidence, examined all the data in this question and concluded that the psalm-singing looked like a picturesque invention. 'Sir Walter', he wrote, in a series of letters to the late William Cowan, now in the possession of the editor of this Supplement, 'makes the Covenanters sing Psalm lxxvi after they had got into their chosen battle-ground. The person who invented the story of their singing on the march probably never tried to set his best foot foremost going down a broken, boggy hillside, and sing at the same time.'

John Gibson Lockhart, in *Peter's Letters to his Kinsfolk* (vol. iii, p. 332), stated that MARTYRS was at that time, about 1819, a great favourite over the west of Scotland, and that it was usually sung in schools to the following words:

> This is the tune the Martyrs sang
> When they, condemned to die,
> Did stand all at the gallows-tree
> Their God to glorify.

Peter Morris, in his description, which follows, of a Scottish sacra-
mental Sabbath, speaks of 'the deep and thrilling harmony' of the
people's untaught voices, 'when they lifted them all up together in
that old tune which immemorial custom has set apart for the last
psalm sung upon this sacred day—a tune which is endeared to them
by the memory of those from whose attachment its designation is
derived, still more than by the low and affecting swell of its own
sad, composing cadences—the "plaintive *Martyrs*, worthy of the
name". The quaint choral falls of this antique melody, breathed by
such a multitude of old and young, diffused a kind of holy charm
over the tall, whispering groves and darkening fields around—a
thousand times more grand and majestic than all the gorgeous stops
of an organ ever wakened in the echoing aisles of a cathedral. There
was a breath of sober, enduring heroism in its long-repeated, melancholy accents—which seemed to fall like a sweet evening dew upon
all the hearts that drank in the sacred murmurs.'

It is possible that the tune MARTYRS, first printed under this name
in the Scottish Psalter of 1615, commemorates the martyrs of the
previous century on account of its association with Psalm li, which
was the psalm which the martyr George Wishart desired to be sung
on the evening before his apprehension in 1546. But it will not fit
the Wedderburn version, in *The Gude and Godlie Ballatis* (see note
on Hymn 174 in this Supplement), quoted by Knox as the one used
on that occasion, which consists of six-line stanzas followed in each
verse by a refrain; nor yet does it fit Whittingham's rendering in
eight eights. It will, however, fit T. Norton's D.C.M. version in
the English Psalter of 1562, if the stanza be divided into two. And
it is rather an interesting point that Norton's psalm is directed in
the English Psalter to be sung to the tune of LAMENTATION (No. I),
and that one line of LAMENTATION is almost exactly the same as the
third line of MARTYRS; there are general resemblances also, suggesting
that MARTYRS might have been partly constructed out of LAMENTA-
TION reduced to the length of a 'common tune' for the 'Martyr's
psalm' and altered in traditional use.

LAMENTATION, in the Aeolian mode, as in Day's Psalter, 1591,
has lines 1, 6, 7, and 8 as follows:

524 JESUS, LORD OF LIFE AND GLORY

AD PERENNIS VITAE FONTEM is said to be from the *Tours Breviary*,
but confirmation of this is lacking.

525 IN THE HOUR OF TRIAL

The original form of DÚN ÁLUINN is as follows:

526 A SAFE STRONGHOLD OUR GOD IS STILL

Dr. James Mackinnon, in his *Luther and the Reformation* (vol. iv, p. 327), refers thus to this hymn: 'In this magnificent challenge of the foe we have the thrilling manifestation of the spirit that carried him and the Reformation to triumph in the struggle with the might and majesty of Rome. It is unquestionably a masterpiece of religious emotion, into which he put, as Lucke expresses it, "the quintessence of his life".'

531 O GOD OF TRUTH, WHOSE LIVING WORD

This hymn, according to Ellerton, 'is obviously suggested by Mr. Maurice's sermon on "The Word of God conquering by Sacrifice" in his volume on *The Doctrine of Sacrifice*'.

The identity of the supposed composer of BLACKBOURN—a Lancashire musician named J. Fish—cannot be determined. This being so, there is probability in the attribution of the tune to Willem Defesch, a Dutch organist of the first half of the eighteenth century, who wrote two oratorios, *Joseph* and *Judith*, a mass, and a variety of instrumental works. The name 'Fish' is probably a corruption of this name.

533 MUCH IN SORROW, OFT IN WOE

The 'Miss Fuller-Maitland' of the *Handbook* note was Frances Sara, afterwards Mrs. John Colquhoun. The story is that her mother showed her Kirke White's fragment, expressing regret that it had not been finished. Frances took it to her room and 'presently brought it back with the 14 lines completed'. Mrs. Colquhoun included the hymn in her collected verses, *Rhymes and Chimes* (1876). Edward Bickersteth was the first to include it in a hymn-book—in his *Christian Psalmody* (1833). It was he who altered the first line to the form in which it appears in most hymnals—'Oft in danger, oft in woe'; he made numerous other changes besides.

534 SOLDIERS OF CHRIST! ARISE

'It seems likely that the words were set going by the melody. In the 1761 tune-book the hymn is set to one of Handel's stirring marches, which requires two 8-line verses for the complete recital of the tune. Altogether it is a *tour de force*.' (F. Luke Wiseman, in *Charles Wesley, Evangelist and Poet*.)

This being so, Dr. Naylor's fine tune, FROM STRENGTH TO STRENGTH, restores the hymn to the 8-line form which Wesley intended for it. The tune was composed for use in Emmanuel College Chapel, Cambridge, about 1902, and was first published in sheet form.

The march referred to is in the opera *Richard the First*. The tune may be found as JERICHO TUNE in *The Methodist Hymnbook*, 819, and also in an abridged form in *Songs of Praise*, 343, under the name MILITES. (See J. T. Lightwood's *Hymn Tunes and their Story*, p. 123.)

536 SAY NOT, 'THE STRUGGLE NOUGHT AVAILETH'

The tune GRACE DIEU, in *The European Psalmist* (1872), where it first appeared, was set to Jane Maurice's hymn 'There is a rest from sin and sorrow'.

549 LORD, IT BELONGS NOT TO MY CARE

The title Baxter gave to this hymn, misquoted in the *Handbook* note, was 'The Concordant Discord of a Broken-healed Heart'. The poem begins:

> My whole, though broken heart, O Lord!
> From henceforth shall be Thine.
> And here I do my vow record:
> This hand, these words, are mine.

The hymn begins with ver. 4 of the original:

> Now it belongs not to my care.

The Church Anthem Book contains an anthem setting of this hymn, by Sir Walford Davies.

552 JESUS IS OUR SHEPHERD

All that can be discovered about the writer of the tune from which GOSHEN was adapted is that her name was Marchel Davis, and that she lived in Dublin. The date of her song is about 1848–50.

GOSHEN is almost identical with Miss Davis's 'Happy Hours of Childhood', but a few more of the notes are dotted in the original, which is reprinted in Kidson and Moffat's *Minstrelsy of Childhood*, 1911. It is a pretty and rather wistful song, beginning:

> Happy hours of childhood,
> Soon they pass away,
> O'er the mount and wild-wood
> Joyous all the day.

Swift those laughing hours,
On light pinions borne,
Pass like summer flowers,
Never to return.

557 HE THAT IS DOWN NEEDS FEAR NO FALL

The air, 'Little Sir William'—on which st. hugh is based will be found in *English County Songs*, p. 86.

559 'TWIXT GLEAMS OF JOY AND CLOUDS OF DOUBT

Of the third mode melody the musical editor of *Songs of Praise Discussed* says: 'It is a remarkable tune, with a nobility and solid grandeur which . . . place it among the greatest melodic conceptions of Tallis's genius. It is the theme of R. Vaughan Williams's *Fantasia for Strings*, where the supreme beauty of the tune is given full value.'

562 O GOD OF BETHEL! BY WHOSE HAND

This was sung at the funeral of David Livingstone, 'brought by faithful hands over land and sea,' in Westminster Abbey, on Saturday, April 18, 1874.

568 LEAD, KINDLY LIGHT

Newman, questioned as to the precise meaning of 'kindly Light', answered: 'There must be a statute of limitation for writers of verse, or it would be quite tyranny if, in an art which is the expression, not of truth, but of imagination and sentiment, one were obliged to be ready for examination on the transient states of mind which came upon one when home-sick, or sea-sick, or in any other way sensitive or excited.' (*Letter to Dr. Greenhill*, Jan. 18, 1879.)

Dykes's tune lux benigna came to the composer as he walked along the Strand—'a curious contrast to the calm Mediterranean night which inspired the words'.

570 O LORD, I SING THY PRAISES

Of killin, Miss Gilchrist says: 'It does not sound to me like a Gaelic air, and in the absence of the 6th degree of the mode it cannot conclusively be called Dorian. It has the Aeolian signature of B♭. Also the Dorian mode is very rare amongst Highland airs; it is a mode belonging to the Lowlands of Scotland and to English folk-music.'

571 THE GOD OF ABRAHAM PRAISE

The Hebrew *Yigdal* which suggested this hymn to Olivers is a confession of faith which is read at the opening of the morning service every day in the Jewish ritual, but is sung to traditional tunes on the Sabbath eve and on the evenings of the Jewish Festivals. It is believed to have been written by Daniel ben Judah Dayyan in 1404, and is founded on the thirteen creeds of Moses ben Maimon. The traditional tunes to which it is sung are many, derived from various countries.

574 CHILDREN OF THE HEAVENLY KING

The tune by Joseph Smith referred to in the *Handbook* note as the possible source of INNOCENTS is given below. Smith set his tune to a child's song called by him 'The Sun', which Miss A. G. Gilchrist found in the collected works of Ann and Jane Taylor (q.v.), under the title 'A Fine Thing'—a sort of poetic riddle (in five verses) of which Smith oddly preferred to give away the answer in his title.

> Who am I with noble face,
> Shining in a clear blue place?
> If to look at me you try,
> I shall blind your little eye.
>
> When my noble face I shew
> Over yonder mountains blue,
> All the clouds away do ride,
> And the dusky night beside. . . .

According to one supposition, Smith's tune fell into the hands of the then anonymous editor of *The Parish Choir* (1846–51), afterwards known to be W. H. Monk, and by him was adapted to a 'Hymn for Innocents' Day' (whence the name of the tune)—a translation of Prudentius's 'Salvete flores martyrum'.

In an article in *The Choir* for April 1929, Miss Gilchrist argued that Monk did not use Smith's tune, but that both drew from a common original, the tune 'Saxony', which was familiar in psalm-tune books from 1791, when it was first printed in Arnold and Callcott's *The Psalms of David for Use in Parish Churches*, down to the latter half of the nineteenth century. SAXONY was an adaptation from the air 'Non vi piacque ingiusti Dei' (One cannot please unjust gods), in Handel's opera *Siroë* (1728); it is made out of the first four bars and later selected phrases of the aria. (Cf. note under Psalter Tunes in this Supplement on 'Heriot's Tune'.)

Another link in the history of INNOCENTS may be found in the air of 'Dear is my little native vale', in *The Edinburgh Musical Miscellany* of 1793, though its precise place in the evolution is not clear. It appeared in an English collection ten years later, and may possibly have furnished the medium through which Smith received his suggestion.

576 WHO WOULD TRUE VALOUR SEE

Although Bunyan may have known Shakespeare's song in *As You Like It*—'Who doth ambition shun'—his own is written in a different metre, a ballad-measure popular in the sixteenth and seventeenth centuries, of which the best-known example to-day is 'O what a plague is love' (Phillida flouts me). See Chappell's *Popular Music* for this and other similar triple-time tunes. Bunyan's stanza is the same as that of the Shakespeare song, except that he does not double the first four lines before coming to his triplet of rhyming lines. Other contemporary songs in this dactylic metre dispense with the triplet, merely doubling the first quatrain, but their tunes are interchangeable. One of these, 'The Valiant Seaman's Happy Return to his True Love', may have helped to suggest Bunyan's opening line, following on Mr. Valiant's speech:

Who would true valour see . . .

MONKS GATE was noted as sung by a Mrs. Verrall, of Monks Gate, near Horsham, Sussex, to a traditional version of the same 'Valiant' or 'Welcome Sailor' ballad, beginning:

Our captain calls all hands
On board to-morrow,
Leaving my dear to mourn
In grief and sorrow.
Dry up those briny tears
And leave off weeping,
So happy may we be
At our next meeting.

It is not impossible that MONKS GATE is a traditional version of the very tune Bunyan had in his mind when he wrote his Pilgrim Song. The 'Valiant Seaman' ballad was directed to be sung to a triple-time tune, 'I am so deep in love: Or, Through the cool shady Woods' (Cupid's Courtesy), preserved in Chappell's *Popular Music of the Olden Time*. The ambiguous and irregular rhythm of MONKS GATE— of which there are other versions in the *Folk-Song Journal*—suggests an origin as a triple-time tune, like others belonging to Elizabethan songs in the Bunyan metre. See *Folk-Song Journal*, vol. iii, pp. 97–8. For MONKS GATE see vol. ii, p. 202.

580 HARK, HARK, MY SOUL! ANGELIC SONGS ARE SWELLING

Sullivan, whether deliberately plagiarizing or not, seems to have borrowed the last four lines of this melody for a chorus in *Patience*.

581 THE SANDS OF TIME ARE SINKING

It was the melody only for the arrangement of which E. F. Rimbault was responsible.

587 THERE IS A HAPPY LAND

The tunes of this hymn and 'Jesus loves me' (660) are both pentatonic, and because of this, our China missionaries find that they are easily learnt by the Chinese, whose attempts to sing the semitones of certain English hymn-tunes are very painful. Chinese music is pentatonic in its system, and these tunes are therefore more akin to the native gapped modes.

592 THERE IS A LAND OF PURE DELIGHT

There is some uncertainty as to the traditional localization of the 'sweet fields beyond the swelling flood' on the shores of Southampton Water. On the one hand T. Wright suggests 'the pleasant meadows near Netley', but on the other, he goes on to say: 'Few cities can boast a fairer landscape than that which greets the tourist when, standing on Southampton Pier, he looks out over the broad waters of the estuary and the swelling uplands, and ample meadows which stretch beyond, as far even as the waving masses of the New Forest.' If the meadows near Netley inspired the line, the poet must have been looking eastward, and the New Forest must be ruled out; if he was thinking of those between the estuary and the Forest, he must have been looking in the opposite direction, and Netley must be ruled out. Julian's suggestion that the Isle of Wight inspired the line can hardly be entertained, for with the fair prospects both east and west, and near at hand, before the poet's eyes, it is not likely that he would find his inspiration beyond them, in an island ten miles or more away.

595 JERUSALEM, MY HAPPY HOME

THIS ENDRIS NYGHT ('endris' meaning 'last') was the tune of a carol beginning:

> Thys endris nygth I saw a sygth,
> A ster as brygth as daye,
> And ever among a maydyn song
> By by, baby, lullay.

A facsimile of the MS. from which it was taken, both words and music, may be seen in the Historical Edition (1904) of *Hymns Ancient and Modern*, p. xxviii.

596 FROM HEAVENLY JERUSALEM'S TOWERS

CRUGYBAR, which does not seem to have appeared in print before 1883, was probably, like JOANNA (q.v.), originally in triple time; but from its use as a funeral hymn, sung at a very slow *tempo*, it has assumed its present form. 'Old Derby' is another example of this development from triple time. In the *Welsh Folk-Song Journal*, vol. ii (1919), p. 128, under the carol 'O deued Pob Cristion', the editor comments on the 'tendency among old singers to divide the lines into short phrases, prolonging the end of each phrase and giving the effect of syncopation'. The carol in question furnishes an example of this way of singing a triple-time air. CRUGYBAR belongs to a group of triple-time folk-tunes in three-bar phrases, suggesting an origin as a dance-air. It is rather like a major form of 'The pretty girl milking her cow', which appears in Ieuan Gwyllt's earlier book as 'Llanarmon'. Cf. also 'Old Derby' and 'Bethel', the latter being set to the same hymn to which CRUGYBAR belongs, in *Canadiau y Cyssegr a'r Teulu*. The original form of CRUGYBAR was probably this:

597-9 BRIEF LIFE IS HERE OUR PORTION

The metre of the original poem has been imitated also by Swinburne:

'O land, without guilt, strong city safe built in a marvellous place,
I cling to thee, ache for thee, sing to thee, wake for thee, watch for thy face.'

See *The Boyhood of Swinburne*, by Mrs. Disney Leith, p. 33.

597 BRIEF LIFE IS HERE OUR PORTION

The tune JABEZ has appeared in various forms since 1839, under the names also of 'Rhuabon', 'Deisyfiod', 'Jamaica', and 'Dewi Sant'. It is a variant of a tune in Nicholas Bennett's *Alawon fy Ngwlad* (Songs of our land), which, without any Welsh title, is called 'The Spanish Minuet'. The South Wales form most nearly resembles JABEZ, the North Wales version, given on the same page (103), being a major version.

601 O GOD, OUR HELP IN AGES PAST

F. J. Gillman, in *The Evolution of the English Hymn* (1927), p. 209, compares Watts's two masterpieces, 'O God, our help' and 'When I survey', thus:

'They both, in a superlative degree, reveal the characteristic features of his best work—its simple strength, its transparency, its hold upon the common mind, its straightforwardness, its accentual and punctuative perfection, and its faithfulness to Scripture. The first has become the great ceremonial hymn of the English nation, and if nothing else had come from his pen, it justifies its author's memorial in Westminster Abbey. The other is more personal, and has more passion.'

Dr. Jowett once asked a tea-party of Balliol and other dons to jot down a small list of the best hymns. It is said that they all returned their papers with one hymn only mentioned, 'O God, our help', each feeling that it fulfilled all the conditions of a perfect hymn.

The tune ST. ANNE no doubt gets its name from St. Anne's, Soho, where Croft was organist when it was composed. Like many other first-class tunes, TALLIS, for instance, it is not wholly original. The first line is a stock phrase which makes frequent appearances in the seventeenth and eighteenth centuries. It is the initial phrase, for example, in two tunes by Henry Lawes in Sandys's *Paraphrase upon the Psalms of David* (1637), and of the first chorus in Handel's sixth Chandos Anthem, 'O praise the Lord' (1734); it is the theme also of Bach's famous organ fugue in E♭, which has therefore, in England, come to be known as 'St. Anne's Fugue'.

605 AT THY FEET, OUR GOD AND FATHER

James Drummond Burns's hymn appeared first in 1861 in *The Family Treasury*, a religious monthly then circulating widely in Scotland, and six years later in his *Psalms and Hymns for Divine Worship*.

608 THE GLORY OF THE SPRING HOW SWEET

The English traditional May Day carol referred to in the *Handbook* note as 'The moon shines bright', is given, as sung by Mrs. Marshall, King's Langley (whence the name of the hymn-tune), in *English County Songs*, p. 108.

612 THE SUMMER DAYS ARE COME AGAIN

This hymn, dated 1859, and entitled 'Summer Rural Gathering' in *Hymns and Verses* (Houghton and Mifflin, 1894), began as follows:

> The sweet June days are come again,
>   With sun and clouds between,
> And, fed alike by sun and rain,
>   The trees grow broad and green;
> Spreads broad and green the leafy tent,
>   Upon whose grassy floor
> Our feet, too long in cities pent,
>   Their freedom find once more.

625 O LORD, BE WITH US WHEN WE SAIL

The adaptation of FARRANT as a hymn-tune was made by Dr. Edward Hodges of Bristol, who arranged it as a common metre tune and sent it to W. H. Havergal for inclusion in his *Old Church Psalmody* (1847).

626 ETERNAL FATHER, STRONG TO SAVE

Of MELITA F. G. Edwards says: 'In the last line but one of each verse the inflected note (F sharp) gives to the word "cry" a piercing and plaintive emphasis, and yet its introduction seems both natural and unrestrained.'

631 GOD SAVE OUR GRACIOUS KING

Mr. J. A. Fuller-Maitland, in his autobiographical *A Door-keeper of Music* (1929), threw light on the history of the tune. 'In editing the catches of Purcell for the Purcell Society', he wrote, 'Squire [i.e. W. Barclay Squire] and I found one written to celebrate the return of the Duke of York (James II) from virtual exile in 1680; and that the words 'God save the King' which occur in it are set to the very same four notes of the tune. The little phrase is obviously used as an allusion to something already familiar, and though the identity of the phrase does not at once strike the eye, yet when the catch was sung at a meeting of the Musical Association at which I reported the discovery, the prominence given to the four notes made it a matter of certainty that the quotation was deliberately made. Before this catch was found, the earliest date for the appearance of the tune we know was 1740 or 1743; as the MS. containing the catch, now in the British Museum, bears as a date of ownership 1681, the song is undoubtedly older than that, since it seems to be quoted in the catch as though the allusion would be recognized by those who heard it. Incidentally, the catch proves that the reference of the song was to the house of Stuart, not to that of Hanover.'

This assignment of a Stuart origin to the hymn may be supported by the line

Send him victorious,

which suggests a reference to the exiled king. In the Jacobite version, extant as engraved on the 'treason glasses' of the Jacobite period, privately used for drinking the 'king's' health, we have the line '*Soon* to reign over us', and a second verse:

God bless the Prince of Wales,
The true-born Prince of Wales,
  Sent us by Thee.
Grant us one favour more,
The king for to restore,
As Thou hast done before
  The familie.

See *The Romance of the White Rose*, 1933, by Grant R. Francis, F.S.A.

634 PRAISE TO OUR GOD, WHOSE BOUNTEOUS HAND

The main source of our knowledge of AGINCOURT SONG is a long parchment roll in the Library of Trinity College, Cambridge. There is another MS. in the Pepys Library, Magdalene College. See J. A. Fuller-Maitland's *A Doorkeeper of Music*.

636 JUDGE ETERNAL, THRONED IN SPLENDOUR

Mr. Archibald Jacob, in his note on PICARDY in *Songs of Praise Discussed*, says that this tune is unlike other French carol tunes used in that book in this respect, that 'there is no childlike mirth or gaiety here, whether the tune be sung fast or slow. In the present instance it must be sung very slowly, when its character appears rather sombre, but at the same time dignified and ceremonious; if, however, it is sung fast, the sombreness changes to fierceness, and though it may suggest a dance, it is a dance of no amenable kind. All tunes change their character, to a certain degree, with a considerable change of speed, but the cleavage here is of a very remarkable nature, and denotes an unusual tune.'

638 O GOD OF EARTH AND ALTAR

Chesterton's hymn appeared originally in Scott Holland's monthly magazine *The Commonwealth*. Knowing nothing of music himself, and unable to tell one tune from another, he told Canon Dearmer that he assumed that AURELIA was the typical tune for hymns, and therefore wrote this hymn in that metre.

639 THESE THINGS SHALL BE

The first hymn-book to include this hymn was *The Methodist Hymn Book* of 1904. It has a place in *The League of Nations Song Book*.

640 AND DID THOSE FEET IN ANCIENT TIME

The first sentence of the first paragraph on p. 222 should read: 'It was suggested to Sir Hubert Parry by Dr. Robert Bridges.'

654 JESUS, TENDER SHEPHERD, HEAR ME

Sir John Stainer told F. G. Edwards, a former editor of *The Musical Times*, that the melody of EVENING PRAYER was founded on the opening theme of Beethoven's Andante in F.

659 WHEN MOTHERS OF SALEM

It should be said for Mr. Hutchings, who wrote this hymn, that he was probably quite unaware that the tune to which he wrote it was originally a German drinking song. The tune is to be found in a collection of social songs, *c.* 1850—W. E. Hickson's *Part Music*—to quite innocuous words beginning:

> O come, come away, from labour now reposing,
>> Let busy care awhile forbear,
>>> O come, come away.

Come, come, our social joys renew,
And there where love and friendship grew
    Let true hearts welcome you,
    O come, come away.

This was obviously the model for at least three early Sunday-school hymns to the same tune (one of them beginning with exactly the same three lines), which are to be found in Brumby's *Gems of Sacred Poetry* (1858), in *Lancashire Sunday School Songs*, and in *The North of England Sunday School Hymnbook*. In this last collection No. 48 is 'The Sunday Scholar's Invitation':

O come, come to school, your teachers join in praises,
    On this happy Pearl of days
    O come, come away.

No. 50 is 'The Child's Welcome to Jesus'—Hutchings's hymn. In the Lancashire book 'O come, come away' is No. 15, with 'Mothers of Salem' set later in the book to the same tune. In Brumby's *Gems* the 'Come, come away' hymn, only, is printed to the tune. From this it seems probable that the *Krambambuli* tune was already in use in North of England Sunday schools when Hutchings wrote his hymn to it, that the hymns of 'Invitation' suggested 'The Child's Welcome to Jesus' for the Wigan anniversary for which it was written, and that all the 'Come, come away' versions were based on Hickson's part-song to the German tune. (For Hickson see biographical note in Handbook.)

661 LORD, A LITTLE BAND AND LOWLY

The tune ROUSSEAU is adapted from the *divertissement* (Scene VIII) in *Le Devin du Village* (The Village Sorcerer), *Intermède* in one Act, words and music by J. J. Rousseau; first played at Fontaine-bleau, Oct. 18, 1752; translated and adapted as *The Cunning Man* by Dr. Burney, and produced at Drury Lane in 1766.

The first vocal adaptation of it appears to have been under the title 'Melissa' to words by Charles James (1788). Mr. James T. Lightwood has recently traced this song under its proper title, 'Sweet Melissa', in the British Museum. It furnishes a valuable link between the *divertissement* air and 'Rousseau's Dream', as J. B. Cramer, with whom this name seems to have originated, published it in his *Songe de J. J. Rousseau, Air varié pour le Forte Piano, arrangé pour les petits Pianos* (Paris, vers 1812; and in England by Chappell in the same year). What Cramer meant by 'Songe' (Dream) is wholly left to the imagination.

In the British Museum copy or catalogue the date 1788 for 'Sweet Melissa' is given with a query. The writer of the words may probably be identified with the Charles James (d. 1821), major and author, who travelled through France during the Revolution (which he upheld), was imprisoned, and died at Boulogne. (See *Dictionary of*

National Biography.) In America the tune as we know it is called 'Days of Absence', from the 'thrice familiar' words set to the tune, which begin:

> Days of absence, sad and dreary,
>   Cloth'd in sorrow's dark array;
> Days of absence, I am weary,
>   She I love is far away.
> Hours of bliss, too quickly vanish'd,
>   When will aught like you return,
> When the heavy sigh be banish'd,
>   When this bosom cease to mourn?

The song is addressed to 'Antoinette', which may be the only colour for the suggestion that Rousseau wrote the words (presumably in French) as well as adapted the tune from his opera. (See *Our Familiar Songs and those who wrote them*, edited by Helen Kendrick Johnson, New York, 1889.) The tune has been known as a hymn-tune in America at least since 1838, when it appeared in *The Christian Lyre* under the name 'Greenville'. It seems never to have been known in America as 'Rousseau's Dream'. 'Sweet Melissa' is as follows:

It is possible that the following hymn-tune, known in earlier American hymn-books as 'Middleton' or 'Opal', and sung to 'Hail, Thou once-despised Jesus', is an independent offshoot from Rousseau's original air:

The first adaptation of the tune to a hymn appears to have been in Thomas Walter's *Companion to Dr. Rippon's Tunes* (1825). It afterwards appeared in *Sacred Melodies* (1843) with the name 'Rousseau' attached to it.

A remarkable resemblance may be noted between this tune and the Scots air, 'Gude e'en to you, Kimmer', in Johnson's *Museum* (No. 523).

673. GOD, WHO CREATED ME

Appeared first in *Love in a Looking-Glass* (1891).

676 PRAISE TO OUR GOD, WHO WITH LOVE NEVER SWERVING

Goss's tune BEDE is an adaptation from the duet 'Cease thy anguish, smile once more' in Handel's oratorio *Athalia*, Part Second, Scene III. Handel's melody is as follows:

679 REVIVE THY WORK, O LORD

CAMBERWELL is by Ralph Harrison. It appeared in vol. i of his *Sacred Harmony* in 1784. The name usually given to it is CAMBRIDGE.

692 THERE IS A FOUNTAIN FILLED WITH BLOOD

Dr. Lowell Mason published a shortened form of Havergal's song-melody in 1850, calling it EVA. It was afterwards named EVAN. The 3/2 form in which Mason rearranged it was as follows, in a halting metre to which as a hymn-composer he was rather addicted.

It appears thus as 'Arranged by Dr. Lowell Mason' in *The Shawm*, 1853. This was evidently the American version—also found in later American tune-books—which Havergal called 'a sad estrangement', preferring to reconstruct his tune himself, if it had to be done, in common time, as it appears in the *Church Hymnary*, except that in Havergal's own arrangement of 1870 each line begins with a semibreve.

Havergal's original air was deliberately composed for 'Burns's Prayer', in what he conceived to be the Scottish manner, and it appears as though he may have taken MARTYRDOM as his model, for his tune is rather like MARTYRDOM the wrong side up.

In the United States the tune is generally sung still in 3/2 time.

The Tonic Sol-fa Reporter of May, 1878, said that at that time the popularity of this tune in Scotland, America, and the Colonies was quite unprecedented.

703 A DEBTOR TO MERCY ALONE

C. J. Abbey, in *The English Church in the Eighteenth Century*, vol. ii, p. 523, has the following criticism: 'Toplady's hymns have many faults. His rhymes are often extremely careless. . . . He is apt to employ a variety of confused metaphors: sometimes he uses expressions which offend by their want of taste; and occasionally he does not scruple to use an Alexander Selkirk metre which is particularly disagreeable to the ear when adapted to sacred subjects. Apart from all question whether statements of peculiar dogmatic views are not prosaic and inappropriate as introduced into a hymn, what solemnity can there be in such a jingle as the following?

> A debtor to mercy alone,
>   Of covenant mercy I sing;
> Nor fear, with Thy righteousness on,
>   My person and offering to bring.'

In a little collection of about sixty hymns edited for use in the morning worship of a girls' school in Bombay which is attended by Moslems, Parsis, and Hindus, as well as Christians, this hymn, rather remarkably, is one of those included.

704 YIELD NOT TO TEMPTATION

If Dr. Palmer's hymn was written in 1868, as is stated in the *Handbook* note, and set to its tune in the same year, the latter would seem to have been merely an adaptation from the following earlier tune, which appeared in Bradbury's *Golden Chain* in 1864, and in the same editor's *New Golden Trio* in 1866, set to a hymn:

> Come, come, sing to the Saviour,
>   Love, love, beams from His eye.
> Haste, then, share in His favour,
>   Worship the Saviour on high.
>   Worship the Saviour (*bis*),
>   Worship the Saviour on high.

727 'Authorized' should be 'Revised'.

HISTORICAL NOTES ON THE PSALTER TUNES NOT INCLUDED IN THE REVISED CHURCH HYMNARY

ABERFELDY first appeared in *The Psalms of David, in Prose and Metre: with the whole Forme of Discipline, and Prayers, according to the Church of Scotland.* (Aberdene: Printed by Edward Raban. 1633.) It is placed there among the Common Tunes, and is named 'Montrosse Tune'. In the 1633 Psalter, printed by Andro Hart's Heirs, it is set without a name to Psalm xxi. The name it now bears appears to have been given to it by H. E. Dibdin (q.v.) in his *Standard Psalm Tune Book* (1851). In its modern form it differs slightly at some points, principally in the inner parts, from that in which it is given in those early psalters.

Like BON ACCORD (q.v.), this tune is an example of what were called 'Tunes in Reports' in the books that first printed them. The name is derived from the French *rapporter*, to carry back, and it is used to describe what musicians now would call a short fugal passage. 'It may have been understood to mean either a *carrying back*, that is, after a passage has been started by one harmonic part, taking it back to the same point and starting it anew by another; or, *carrying again*, that is, repeating the passage by the parts in succession. Or, if the term referred to echoing, answering, or what is now called Imitation, the idea is still the same.' (Dr. Neil Livingston, *The Scottish Metrical Psalter of A.D. 1635, reprinted in full from the Original Work, with Dissertations, Notes, and Facsimiles.* 1864.)

In both these tunes the melody is given to the 'Trebbles', contrary to the universal practice in those times, which is followed in every other instance in the early psalm-books, of assigning the 'Church Part' or melody to the tenors.

ARNOLD first appeared in *The Psalms of David for the Use of Parish Churches. The Music selected, adapted, and composed by Dr. Arnold . . . assisted by J. W. Callcott* (1791). It was there set to Psalm xv, and arranged so that the first two lines should be sung as a duet by first and second trebles, the same lines repeated also as a duet by tenor and bass, and the third and fourth lines sung in full chorus. It is first found in Scotland, in the form in which it is now used, in Robert Gilmour's *Psalm Singer's Assistant* (n.d., but before 1793).

ASPURG (also known as 'Kornthal') is from *Vierstimmige Gesänge der evangelischen Kirche* (Stuttgart, 1825). It is there set to the hymn 'Singt unserm Herrn ein dankvoll Lied'.

AYNHOE, though commonly attributed to Dr. Nares (q.v.), does not appear in the collections of Smart and Riley, to which he contributed. It is an altered form of a tune named HAYNOR, which Dibdin ascribed to Christopher Clark, from *Vocal Harmony* (1745), and which is found also, but without any composer's name, in Abraham Milner's *Psalm Singer's Companion* (1751).

BLOXHAM is from Aaron Williams's *New Universal Psalmodist*, (1770), where it is set to Dr. Watts's version of Psalm xxxiv. The melody there is as follows:

BON ACCORD is from the edition of the Scottish Psalter published in 1625 in Aberdeen by Edward Raban. The exact title of this edition cannot be given, as the title-page is lacking in both of the two copies which alone are known to be in existence. The date and the printer's name are given on the last page. This tune is headed 'Bon Accord for the xii. Psalm'. It is harmonized 'in Reports' like ABERFELDY (q.v.). In the same form it appears again in Hart's Edinburgh Psalter of 1635, but with some slight differences in the parts.

BREDON is from *The Church Psalter and Hymnal*, edited by the Rev. Edward Harland, M.A. (1855).

CANNONS (always spelt CANONS in Handel's time) is one of the three tunes composed by Handel out of friendship for the Wesleys. Its original title was 'The Invitation', because of its being written for the hymn 'Sinners, obey the Gospel word'. Canons was the palace, nine miles out of London, near Edgware, where 'the magnificent' Duke of Chandos lived in almost royal splendour, and where for a time Handel was his chapel-master and wrote the famous Chandos Anthems and Te Deums, as well as *Esther* and *Acis and Galatea*. See note on Hymn 135 in this Supplement.

CAROLINE first appeared in *The Seraph: A Selection of Psalm and Hymn Tunes, many of them original, for four voices* (Glasgow, 1827). This book was edited and published by John Robertson, who was a teacher of vocal and instrumental music in Glasgow, and who had previously (1814) published *A Selection of the best Psalm and Hymn Tunes, some of which are original, in four parts: adapted to the various Metres used in the Established Churches, Chapels, and Dissenting Congregations in Scotland.*

CAROLINE is one of thirteen tunes in *The Seraph* which are starred as original and 'the private property' of Robertson. It bears no composer's name, although Hugh Wilson, who wrote it, is named as composer of MARTYRDOM.

The tune in its original form had a 'repeat' for the fourth line, as below. The omission of it, while an improvement for present-day use, robs the tune of a good deal of its character, which hardly deserves the adjective 'insipid' which T. L. Hately applied to it.

Our life con - tains a . . thou - sand springs,

And dies if one be gone; Strange that a

harp of thou - sand strings Should keep in

tune so long, Should keep . . . in tune so long.

The verse set under this tune is one of the practice-rhymes of Scottish psalmody in the first half of the nineteenth century, after the precentor had acquired a 'band', to sing in parts. These verses were invented as a substitute for the sacred words to which otherwise the 'band' would rehearse its more secular tunes. These rhymes, as printed in tune-books, were of a moral rather than a religious character—such sacred words as 'God' and 'Christ' being excluded—and were composed not only to sing to long, short, and common measure, but to suit major and minor modes (one for each measure and class) and worded accordingly. They would seem to have been the amateur efforts of the precentor, whose ear in the case above (C.M., Minor Mode) did not tell him that 'long' was not a proper rhyme for 'gone'. These psalmody rhymes have been extensively parodied, but authentic examples are known that are banal enough in character. See the rhyme quoted under MARTYRS in this Supplement.

CHICHESTER is from Ravenscroft's *The Whole Booke of Psalmes . . . composed into 4 parts by sundry Authors* (1621).

COLCHESTER appeared in *A Compleat Melody; or, The Harmony of Zion. . . .* By William Tans'ur. (Preface dated September 29, 1734.) There it is set to Psalm cl, and headed 'Colchester Tune. Composed in Four Parts. W.T.' Whether the initials were intended to indicate that the tune was an original one by Tans'ur, or only that he arranged it, is uncertain.

In its original form the tune was as below:

CONSOLATION (also called EMMANUEL or IMMANUEL) is an adaptation from the theme of the Finale of a Piano Quartet of Beethoven, in E♭ major.

CORONA was written by Mrs. Raymond Barker for *Catholic Hymns. Set to Music by the Composer of Hymns of the Eastern Church* (1868). It is there set to the hymn entitled 'The Crown of Thorns', beginning 'From circlets starred with many a gem'.

COVENTRY appeared in Christopher Smart's *Translation of the Psalms of David* (1765). Poor Kit Smart had two years before this book was published been confined in a madhouse. Dr. Johnson said: 'I did not think he ought to be shut up. His infirmities were not noxious to society. He insisted on people praying with him: and I'd as lief pray with Kit Smart as any one else. Another charge was that he did not love linen; and I have no passion for it.' Garrick gave a performance for Smart's benefit, and, when this translation of the Psalms was published, among the names of subscribers appeared those of Gray, Cowper, Akenside, Churchill, Sterne, Smollett, and Hogarth. He was much loved, but foolish and improvident; he died in the debtors' prison of the King's Bench. Deeply religious, he wrote kneeling. His *Song to David*, composed in the asylum, Sir Edmund Gosse declared to be 'a portent of beauty and originality', and Browning, in his *Parleyings*, says it 'stations Smart on either hand with Milton and with Keats'.

CRIMOND appeared in *The Northern Psalter*, edited by William Carnie, Aberdeen, 1872. This Psalter began by the issue of a series of *Fly Leaves of Psalm and Hymn Tunes*, the first part appearing in 1859. Each number consisted of a lithographed four-paged penny sheet, containing seven tunes, old and new. The lithographing was well done, and the sheets sold in thousands. From them the *Northern Psalter* was in due time compiled. (See biographical note on David Grant.) The tune is set in that Psalter to the hymn 'I am the Way, the Truth, the Life'.

DRUMCLOG appeared in *The Sacred Harp*, published by Robert Burns in Glasgow in 1840; also in *Cameron's Selection of Sacred Music* (Glasgow, G. & J. Cameron, 1852). The preface of the latter says: 'It has been carefully compiled from *The Sacred Harp*, the property of the publishers, which has been universally pronounced *The Classic Standard of Scottish Psalmody*, not only by the entire Scottish press, but by the most eminent practical musicians. . . . Many popular tunes are inserted which were not published in *The Sacred Harp*, and several others are now issued for the first time by permission of the composers.' The tune appeared also in the 1848 and later editions of Mitchison's *Selection of Sacred Music*, which was published in 1834 and enlarged from time to time. All these books give the tune as by Matthew Wilson (q.v.). The tune was a great favourite in the west of Scotland, especially to the 23rd Psalm, until the issue of official Psalters and hymn-books, in which it was not included, led to its falling out of use.

Readers of William Black's novel, *A Daughter of Heth*, will remember the description in chapter xxi, of how Coquette, the heroine of the story, played this tune on board the *Caroline* in Oban Bay. She played first 'the clear, and sweet, and melancholy cadence of Mendelssohn's gondola song. The empty silence of the bay seemed to grow full of this rich and harmonious music. . . . But suddenly she changed the key, and with sharp and powerful chords struck out the proud and ringing melody of "Drumclog". The old Scotch psalm-tune stirred the Whaup, as a trumpet might stir the heart of a dragoon. He rose to his feet, and drew a long breath, as if the plaintive gondola-music had been stifling him.

'"What a grand tune that Drumclog is," he said. "It means business. I dare say the old troopers sang it with their teeth set hard, and their hands on their musket-barrels."'

Later in the story, in chapter xlix, there is a description of Coquette playing the tune in Airlie Manse (supposed to be Stevenston Manse, Ayrshire): 'She seldom opened the piano, and when she did, Drumclog was no longer a martial air, but a plaintive wail of grief.'

Black evidently supposed that the name of the tune implied some historical connexion with the Covenanters; in such wise do accepted traditions arise. By some it has been suggested that the tune in his mind was another, which also has been supposed to be connected with the Covenanters (it has been described as 'partly borrowed from an old Covenanting melody'), with equally little foundation—the tune MARTYRDOM, which appeared in *The Seraph* in 1827 as 'Drum-clog'. It was also known as 'Fenwick', from the parish in which Hugh Wilson composed it, about the end of the eighteenth century. But these names for it were forgotten, and it was universally known as MARTYRDOM, by the mid-nineteenth century. And that is the time about which the events of Black's story are supposed to have taken place. He is not likely to have mistaken the tune.

Black was born in Glasgow in 1841, and did not settle in London till 1864. *A Daughter of Heth* was published in 1871. Its period is round about the 'fifties: 'not earlier than 1855, not later than 1869, probably about 1860', says the Rev. James Mearns in an interesting article in *The Choir*, from which the facts here detailed are taken. At that time there were no official tune-books. Precentors used such Glasgow tune-books as those named above, or manuscript copies of tunes that were in use. The books most likely to have been in use in the churches with which Black was familiar were these; it may reasonably be concluded therefore that this was the tune that was in his mind.

DUKE'S TUNE appeared in *The CL Psalmes of David*, the edition of the first Scottish Psalter published in Edinburgh by Andro Hart in 1615. This was one of the first set published of what were called *Common Tunes*, that is, tunes not attached to any particular psalm, but usable with any psalm in common metre. In this Psalter they were grouped together under the title, 'The XII Common Tunes, to the which all Psalmes of eight syllables in the first line, and sixe in the next may be sung'. (See article in *Handbook* on Early Metrical Psalters.) This tune is so obviously a piece of cobblery that its disuse is not surprising. Of its twenty-eight notes the first five are identical with 'Tallis', and four of its second section and the last thirteen with 'Winchester'.

EATINGTON is from the third edition of Playford's *The Divine Companion; or, David's Harp New Tun'd* (1709), where it bears no name. It is set there to Psalm cxvi, 'I love the Lord because he heard'. It is the third of a group headed thus: 'This Hymn and the following Three Psalms sett by Docter Crofts'. The original was in two parts, and in the key of B♭. In the same book a tune by Jeremiah Clark appears to 'A Morning Hymn. Awake, my soul', the first line of which is exactly the same as the first line of this tune. The similarity will also be remarked between this tune and lines 1 and 3 of Clark's 'St. Magnus'. Eatington (now Ettington) was Croft's birthplace.

EDEN is from W. H. Havergal's *A Hundred Psalm and Hymn Tunes* (1859). It had been composed, however, in 1845, and must have found its way in manuscript across the Atlantic shortly afterwards, for Lowell Mason was using it there, under the name 'St. Nicholas', in April, 1847. In April of that year he wrote thus to Havergal about it: 'I have lately introduced into my choir, and sing with admirable effect, your tune "St. Nicholas". The effect of it was truly magnificent. . . . I have never heard anything come nearer to my *beau ideal* of Choral Music than did the singing of this tune on a fine Sabbath morning, in a Church filled with people. It made a deep impression.' (Havergal's *Psalmody and Century of Chants*, 1870.) The present setting is not Havergal's.

EFFINGHAM is clearly a derivative from 'Crasselius' (q.v., in *Handbook*): *Musicalisch Hand-Buch der Geistlichen Melodien à Cant. et Bass.* (Hamburg, 1690.)

EGHAM is attributed to Dr. William Turner (q.v.) by Dibdin in his *Standard Psalm Tune Book* (1852), and, doubtless on this authority, by Dr. E. J. Hopkins in *The Temple Tune Book, Division I*, but in neither case is there any indication of the source. It is not found in any of the collections to which Turner himself is known to have contributed.

FELIX is founded on a phrase in the chorus 'He stirreth up the Jews' in Mendelssohn's unfinished oratorio *Christus* (Op. 97, Posthumous Works, No. 26), first performed at the Birmingham Musical Festival, 1852. The phrase is as follows:

The tune first appeared under the name BALTIC, in Lowell Mason's *The Hallelujah* (1854), and may be assumed to be his composition.

GENEVA is a modification, of a kind too long customary in Scotland, of PSALM XLII (see Hymn 359 in R.C.H., and note thereon in the *Handbook*), which was composed or adapted by Louis Bourgeois, for Psalm xlii in the Genevan French Psalter of 1551. The Scottish Psalter of 1564, following the Anglo-Genevan Psalter of 1561, set it to Psalm xxvii. It is included in the present Psalter in this form because it has still a measure of use among those who sing the first version of Psalm cxxxvi. Now that the noble original tune is again available, GENEVA will doubtless gradually be disused.

GLENLUCE is No. XX of the Common Tunes in the Scottish Psalter of 1635.

HARINGTON was originally written as a glee for three voices under the title 'Retirement', to words of which the first of three verses is as follows:

> Beneath the silent rural cell
> Of innocence and peace,
> With sage retirement let me dwell
> And taste each home-felt bliss.

The original form of the music was this:

HEREFORD (also called Tranmere, Christchurch, or Psalm xlvii) is from *Sixteen Psalms selected from the Rev. Mr. Merrick's New Version. Set to Music by W. Hayes* (1774), where it is set to the version of Psalm xlvii: 'Arise, ye people, clap the hand'. Hayes says that it is to be played 'on the swelling organ'. In its original form lines 5 and 6 of the tune are as follows:

The Rev. James Merrick, M.A. (1720–69), a Fellow of Trinity

College, Oxford, published at Reading in 1765 *The Psalms of David Translated or Paraphrased in English Verse.* Curiously, only a few of his versions were divided into stanzas. In 1797 the Rev. W. D. Tattersall repaired the omission by publishing Merrick's work 'Divided into stanzas for parochial Use, and paraphrased in such language as will be intelligible to every capacity . . . with a suitable Collect to each Psalm from the Works of Archbishop Parker'. Merrick had vainly tried to obtain the royal sanction for his book; Tattersall was more fortunate: his book, under sanction of the King, was introduced into Weymouth Parish Church in 1804. Both in the Church of England and among Nonconformists a number of Merrick's paraphrases, which Dr. Julian stigmatized as 'weak and verbose', were long in use, and some, chiefly in the form of centos, survived into modern hymn-books. From the newer collections they have disappeared.

HERIOT'S TUNE takes its name from George Heriot's Hospital, Edinburgh. Its first traceable appearance was in *A New Collection of Vocal Music, containing Church Tunes, Anthems, and Songs, for the use of the several Hospitals of this City. By Andrew Lawrie, Teacher of these Hospitals and Writing Master* (Edinburgh, 1780). Lawrie in his Preface says: 'Besides Church tunes I have brought into this collection the several tunes and anthems usually sung on George Heriot's day [the first Monday in June], to which I have added more: and after that, a good number of songs . . . which persons of the chastest ear and strictest character may hear without being offended; and would to God that none but inoffensive songs, such as these, were ever heard in any company; and that all indecent and licentious songs were hissed and banished from mankind, as being more infectious and hurtful than the plague.'

In this volume there are three 'George Heriot's Tunes', one of them being the present one.

A successor to this book was published in *A Collection of Vocal Music, containing Church Tunes, Anthems, and Songs, for the use of the several Hospitals of this City* (Edinburgh, 1807). The editor of this book was Alexander McDonald (q.v.), then joint music-master with his father in the Hospitals. He also gives three so-called 'George Heriot's Tunes'. One is the tune named 'Saxony', which was an adaptation of an air in Handel's opera *Siroë* (1728), and which, from the time of its introduction into Scotland in 1820 in Dr. Andrew Thomson's *Sacred Harmony*, remained in high favour in Scotland for half a century. (See note on INNOCENTS under Hymn 574 in this Supplement.) A second is apparently an amateur's production with its last line taken straight from the tune MANCHESTER. The third is the present tune, which, as it alone appears in both the books here mentioned, appears to be the only one with any claim to be traditional. Its origin is unknown.

HERMON has the 'plaintive grace' which characterizes most of Jeremiah Clark's tunes, reflecting the subdued melancholic strain in his spirit. It does not suggest the triumphant joy of Eastertide, yet it first appeared in Henry Playford's *The Divine Companion; or, David's Harp New Tun'd* (1708), set to *A Hymn for Easter Day*, which began:

> If angels sung a Saviour's birth
>   On that auspicious morn,
> We well may imitate their mirth
>   Now He again is born.

Playford gives the second half of the tune, which is unnamed by him, in this form:

HOWARD, though attributed to Dr. Samuel Howard in Scotland during the last hundred years and more, was not composed by him. The name doubtless gave rise to the mistake. Its first known appearance was in John Wilson's *A Selection of Psalm Tunes, Sanctuses, Doxologies, &c., for the use of the Congregation of St. Mary's Church, Edinburgh* (1825). There no composer's name is given. In books published in 1840 and 1854 it is ascribed to Sir John Andrew Stevenson (q.v.), but with what reason does not appear. In the *Wesleyan Tune Book* of 1877 it is called DUBLIN, ascribed to Stevenson, and printed 'by permission of H. H. Bemrose'. This ascription is repeated in *The Methodist Hymn-Book* of 1933, but Mr. Lightwood, in his *The Music of the Methodist Hymn-Book*, says that it 'lacks corroboration'.

HUDDERSFIELD is one of thirty-three tunes contributed by Martin Madan (q.v. in *Handbook*) to *A Collection of Psalm and Hymn Tunes never Published before. Edited by Martin Madan.* (1769). In this book, known as the *Lock Collection* (q.v. in *Handbook*) it bears its present name, and is set to the hymn beginning:

> My hiding-place, my refuge, tower,
>   And shield art Thou, O God.

In its original form the second half of the tune is as follows:

Historical Notes on the Psalter Tunes

ICONIUM, though traditionally attributed to Dr. James Nares (q.v. in *Handbook*), is not found in any collection to which he is known to have contributed, nor in any collection earlier than 1843. In that year it appeared in *The Sacred Harmony of St. Andrew's Church, Edinburgh, in four vocal parts, with Accompaniment for the Organ or Pianoforte* (1843). Intended as a supplement to R. A. Smith's collections, which were then in very general use, this book contains forty-six tunes, two of which bear the name of Adam Ramage, who had been precentor of the church since 1838 and remained so after the Disruption. Several of the tunes are by John Thomson, Professor of Music in Edinburgh University, who was a son of Dr. Andrew Thomson (q.v.).

INVOCATION is from *Sacred Music . . . sung in St. George's Church, Edinburgh. Edited by R. A. Smith* (Edinburgh, 1825). It was composed for the psalm with which it is inseparably associated —Psalm xliii, vv. 3 to 5. This psalm has from time immemorial been used in the approach to Holy Communion. It has its fixed place there in the Roman Mass, and doubtless its use at the beginning of the Scottish Communion Service is an unrealized inheritance from pre-Reformation days.

This ancientry of use might suggest the propriety of wedding the psalm to a tune in the great tradition which goes back to the Reformation period. There is no more Scottish tune than MARTYRS, for example; it has come down from 1615, and would be singularly appropriate in character and spirit to this psalm. But though INVOCATION has held the field for no more than a century, and is a survival from a time when repeating tunes had a vogue which they have long since lost, it still holds a place in the affections of Scottish people from which it is not likely soon to be driven.

KILSYTH is an adaptation from the chorale *Allein zu Dir Herr Jesu Christ*, which, according to *The Chorale Book for England* (1865), was published first as a broadside at Nürnberg in 1541, and afterwards in *Geistliche Lieder*, Second Part (Leipzig, 1545). The original tune was as follows, but see also Bach's splendid version of it in Dr. Sanford Terry's *J. S. Bach's Four-Part Chorales*.

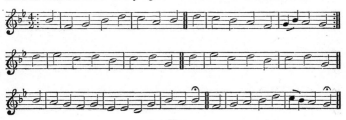

KING'S NORTON by Jeremiah Clark is from Playford's *The Divine Companion; or, David's Harp New Tun'd, &c.* (1708), where it is set to 'An Hymn for Good-Fryday' beginning, 'No songs of Tryumph now be sung'. It is a tune of much attraction, like all that Clark wrote, but the difficulty with which it confronts the average singer in lines 3 and 4 will probably limit its use. 'The whole melody', says Mr. Archibald Jacob in *Songs of Praise Discussed*, 'is reminiscent of many of this composer's small pieces for the harpsichord.'

LANGHOLM is from *The Psalms of David, for the Use of Parish Churches* (1791), edited by Dr. Arnold and Dr. Callcott. There, under the name 'Lancaster', it is set to Psalm xc.

LAWES (PSALM XLVIII) is from *A Paraphrase upon the Psalmes of David. By G[eorge] S[andys]. Set to new Tunes for private Devotion. And a thorow Base, for Voice or Instrument. By Henry Lawes* (1637). Sandys (1577–1643) was son of an Archbishop of York, a Gentleman of the Privy Chamber to Charles I, Treasurer for a time to the colony of Virginia, and a poet, according to Dryden, 'ingenious and learned, the best versifier of a former age'. A few of his versions are found still in modern hymn-books. On Lawes's tunes see note on Hymn 297 in this Supplement.

LINCOLN is from Ravenscroft's *The Whole Booke of Psalmes* (1621), where it is set to Psalms vii and lvi, and described as an 'English' tune, without the composer's name. It is typical of the uninteresting, rather dull music for which too many of Ravenscroft's unnamed composers were responsible.

LIVERPOOL first appeared in *Divine Harmony; being a Collection in Score of Psalms and Anthems, composed by the most eminent masters . . . Selected and . . . Revised by R. Langdon* (1774), where it bears no name, and is set to Psalm viii. It received its name from Ralph Harrison in the second volume of his *Sacred Harmony, or, a Collection of Psalm Tunes, Ancient & Modern* (vol. i, 1784; vol. ii, 1791). Robert Wainwright, who composed it, a Manchester man, died in 1782 in Liverpool, where he was for the last seven years of his life organist of the church which later became the cathedral; hence Harrison's choice of names for this tune and the next. The first form of the melody was this:

MANCHESTER first appeared in Richard Langdon's book, named above as the source of LIVERPOOL; it was set to Psalm ciii. Harrison gave it its name in the second volume of his *Sacred Harmony*. As Wainwright wrote it, it ran thus:

MANCHESTER was christened CHARMOUTH in America when it first appeared there in 1798, and many books in this country have given the tune under that name.

MELROSE is from *The Psalmes of David in Prose and Meeter. With their whole Tunes in foure or mo parts, and some Psalmes in Reports. Whereunto is added many godly Prayers, and an exact Kalendar for xxv. yeeres to come. Printed at Edinburgh by the Heires of Andrew Hart, Anno Dom. 1635.* This was by far the most important of all the editions of the first Scottish Metrical Psalter. It is the only one in which the Proper Tunes, printed at the head of the psalms, are harmonized throughout; it contains also thirty-one Common Tunes, of which the present one is No. 24; and it gives, in addition, eight tunes harmonized 'in reports', as described under ABERFELDY. The usefulness of this edition was of brief duration, for it went out of use only fifteen years after publication, owing to the present *Psalter in Metre*, authorized for use in 1650, substituting for the old text, which had been in use since 1564, a new one which was metrically unsuitable for most of the old tunes.

MILTON is American. Lowell Mason published it under the name 'Kinlock', in 1854, in his *The Hallelujah*, and it quickly found favour in Scotland.

As an illustration of a phase of Scottish Church life and character that has now almost entirely vanished, it may be recorded that to many of a past generation in the north of Scotland this tune was known as *Kitty's Retreat*. 'Kitty' was one of those stalwarts who were always ready to lift up a standard of testimony against anything in the nature of what they considered to be innovations in public worship. Whenever the precentor in the church which she attended gave out MILTON with its broken rhythm, it was a fearful joy among the younger portion of the congregation to see her rise in her place—fifty years ago in the North people sat during the singing, as they do in Germany to-day—and at once make for the door, scattering hats and umbrellas and anything else that happened to impede her progress out of church.

MORVEN appeared in *The Edinburgh Sacred Harmony, for the Use of Churches and Families, consisting of Psalm and Hymn Tunes, Doxologies, Thanksgivings, and Dismissions*, a work issued in parts, at quarterly intervals, by R. A. Smith (q.v.). About ten parts were published; it was not completed when Smith died. This tune appeared set to Psalm cxlii in No. vi, and was described as an 'Ancient Scottish Melody' as SELMA also was; but T. L. Hately (q.v.), who was a member of Smith's choir in St. George's, Edinburgh, held that Smith composed them both.

There is not much room for doubt that this tune, like SELMA and MARTYRDOM (q.v.), is of folk-ballad origin. R. A. Smith was no doubt wise in his day in not announcing the sources of any of the three by name, though their associations were harmless enough. MORVEN suggests one of the numberless tunes sung to 'Barbara Allen', and it has the characteristic rising cadence at the end of the second line found in many of them. It is here set below a 'Barbara Allen' tune, after its reduction (or reversion) to folk-rhythm, for comparison. The 'Barbara Allen' tune (hexatonic) is from Sussex, as noted in 1906 by Miss A. G. Gilchrist.

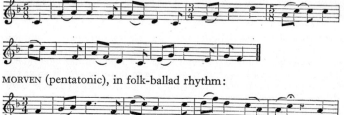

MORVEN (pentatonic), in folk-ballad rhythm:

The latter is quite as like the former as many 'Barbara Allen' variants are to each other. Numerous traditional Scottish tunes in the same metrical form belong to such ballads as 'The Dowie Dens of Yarrow' and 'Geordie', so it is uncertain to what particular ballad R. A. Smith may have heard MORVEN, in its original form, sung.

The name MORVEN is sometimes, but mistakenly, understood to be taken from the beautiful district so named in Argyll. Like SELMA, it is derived from Macpherson's *Ossian*, in which Selma is the capital of the country called Morven. 'I beheld thy towers, O Selma, the oaks of thy shadowed wall.' It is sometimes stated also that Morven is an anglicized form of 'Mor Bean, signifying the hill country or highlands'. Dr. Neil Ross of Laggan, the Celtic scholar, thus dismisses that idea: 'The district in Argyll known as Morven is in Gaelic Marairne. Mór-bheinn would mean a big mountain, if that form were used; but it is not so used. As a rule in Gaelic the adjective comes after the noun, except occasionally in poetic usage. The ordinary form is Beinn-mhór, which is anglicized in Benmore in Mull and Benmore in Assynt. We may dismiss the hill etymology for Morven.

'The simple fact is that Macpherson, like Dickens, had a faculty for coining new names. Neither Morven nor Selma occurs in the genuine Ossianic remnants. The names were pure inventions of Macpherson. In his day, a century and a half ago, his *Ossian* was taken for the real article, and his fine-sounding names were popular. It is not surprising that even psalm-tunes composed in that period should be called by such lovely, mystical but mythical names. They are poetic merely.'

NEWARK appeared anonymously in Nathaniel Gawthorn's *Harmonia Perfecta: a Compleat Collection of Psalm Tunes in Four Parts . . . Taken from the Most Eminent Masters, chiefly from Mr. Ravenscroft* (1730).

NORWICH is from *The Whole Booke of Psalmes . . . Composed into four parts by sundry Authors . . . Newly corrected and enlarged by Tho. Ravenscroft* (1621), where it is set to Psalms v, lv, and cii, the harmony being by John Milton, father of the poet. It is named there 'Norwich tune', and is classed among English Tunes in the index. The last line of the original runs thus:

OLD 29TH is from what is popularly known as *John Knox's Genevan Service Book* (1556), so called because it was used by Knox while he was a minister of the congregation of Marian exiles at Geneva from 1556 to 1559. The full title is *The Forme of Prayers and Ministration of the Sacraments, &c., used in the Englishe Congregation at Geneva . . . Geneva, 1556*. It originated really at Frankfort, where it was drawn up for a similar congregation of exiles, but not found acceptable to them and never used. Because the Genevan congregation adopted it, it was known as the Order of Geneva. In its completed form it was adopted by the Church of Scotland in 1564 as its *Book of Common Order*. The first part was liturgical. The second contained metrical versions of the psalms with the following title, *One and Fiftie Psalmes of David in Englishe Metre, whereof 37 were made by Thomas Sternholde and the rest by others, &c*. The 'others' were John Hopkins, whose name is associated with Sternhold's in connexion with the first English Metrical Psalter, and William Whittingham, who married Calvin's sister, and in later life became

Dean of Durham. Each was responsible for seven of the additions to Sternhold's thirty-seven.

Each of the fifty-one is furnished with a tune. The present one is that set to Psalm xxix. Who the musicians were who contributed these tunes, and who was responsible for the selection and arrangement of them, there is no means of knowing; but both English and Scottish musicians were among the most devoted adherents of the Reformation, and possibly some of these among the exiles in Geneva supplied the music. The fact that this tune was retained in all subsequent Scottish editions, but appeared in none of the English, suggests the possibility that it came from a Scottish composer.

OLD 68TH is from John Day's *Whole Booke of Psalmes, collected into Englysh metre by T. Starnhold, I. Hopkins, and others: conferred with the Ebrue, with apt notes to synge thē withal: Faithfully perused and alowed according to the ordre appointed in the Quenes maiesties Iniunctions. Imprinted at Lōdon by Iohn Day, dwelling ouer Aldersgate . . . An. 1562.* This is important as the first complete edition of the English Metrical Psalter.

With the first two lines of the tune in the original, as follows, compare those of OLD 100TH:

The seventh line also varies from the present form, thus:

In the rare 1562 (English) Psalter Psalm c is not given in Kethe's now familiar version, but in another, anonymous, which begins 'In God the Lorde be glad and lyght'. No tune is given with it, but a marginal direction says: 'Sing this as the lxvii'. This is a misprint for 'lxviii'. The tune given with lxviii is the present one. Major G. A. Crawford, an unrivalled authority on Reformation psalmody, remarked: 'It was a not uncommon practice of the old writers to construct new tunes by adding different terminations to the same fragment of older melody. The strain with which the "Old Hundredth" commences seems to have been very popular from this point of view.'

OLD 124TH appeared first in the book which gave us OLD 100TH, *Pseaumes octante trois de David, mis en rime francoise. A savoir quarante neuf par Clement Marot, . . . Et trente quatre par Theodore de Besze. . . . A Geneve, 1551.* The psalm to which this tune is set and which gives it its name was one of the thirty-four by Beza.

The English version of the words was by William Whittingham, who, as will be seen from a comparison of the first verses, closely followed his original. Thus Beza:

> Or peut bien dire Israel maintenant,
> > Si le Seigneur pour nous n'eust point esté,
> > Si le Seigneur nostre droit n'eust porté,
> Quand tout le monde a grand' fureur venant,
> Pour nous meurtrir dessus nous s'est jetté.

Here is Whittingham's translation:

> Now Israel may say and that truely,
> > If that the Lord had not our cause maintaind,
> > If that the Lord had not our right sustain'd,
> When all the world against us furiouslie
> Made their uproares, and said wee should all die.

Not only in these last two lines, but at many other points, the Scottish revisers who produced our present version in 1650 greatly strengthened Whittingham's version.

The glorious tune, one of the dearest of all to Scottish hearts, differed from the present form. Here is the tune as it originally stood:

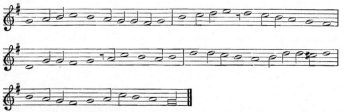

In *The English Hymnal* the tune is set to two sets of verses, written *ad hoc* to make the tune available; one is by the late Canon T. A. Lacey, and the other, a version of a hymn of Prudentius, by Canon Percy Dearmer. In *Songs of Praise* a better, but still unsatisfactory set is provided in Clifford Bax's 'Turn back, O Man, forswear thy foolish ways'. This was written by him in 1916 for Gustav Holst, who wished to use the tune for a motet, which, as now published, has become widely known through the wireless. The first verse runs:

> Turn back, O Man, forswear thy foolish ways.
> Old now is Earth, and none may count her days,
> > Yet thou, her child, whose head is crowned with flame,
> > Still wilt not hear thine inner God proclaim—
> 'Turn back, O Man, forswear thy foolish ways.'

In *Farewell, my Muse* (1932), in which Bax published his verses, he says, 'The regular structure of these verses and the large number of long monosyllables were necessitated by the form of the music.' Scotland is fortunate in having the perfect words provided for the great tune in Whittingham's rugged version of the Psalm, to which it is so closely wedded that to sing it to anything else seems to the Scotsman little short of profanation, for the association has remained unbroken since the Reformation. This fact is remarkable, for though the Scottish Reformers were deeply indebted to the Church of Geneva as regards both the words and the music of their first metrical Psalter, this is the solitary instance in which the same psalm and tune have remained inseparable in the Churches of Calvin and Knox.

Several historic episodes in which psalm and tune together played a part deserve to be recorded.

One is Genevan. It relates to one of the last attempts made by the Dukes of Savoy to reconquer the town of Geneva and crush the Protestant movement. It took place in 1602, and is known as the *Escalade*. The attack was repulsed by the bravery of the citizens. As soon as the enemy was driven off and peace was restored, Beza, then eighty years of age, returned thanks for the victory, and gave out this psalm to be sung to this melody (in Geneva singing in harmony was forbidden). Ever since, the same rite has been observed each year on the 12th of November, the anniversary of the deliverance; and on a monument erected to commemorate it, one of the reliefs represents the aged Reformer at the door of the cathedral, giving out the psalm. This episode is vividly portrayed in Stanley Weyman's novel *The Long Night*.

The second incident is Scottish. John Durie, one of the ministers of Edinburgh, was banished from the city in June, 1582, 'for his plean speitches against the Duc [of Lennox] and proceedings of the Court'. In the August following he was allowed to return. The description of his triumphal entry into the city, as given by Calderwood, has often been quoted; here is the account of it by James Melvill in his *Diary*, upon which Calderwood drew in writing his *History*: 'Jhone Durie gat leiue to ga ham to his awin flok of Edinbruche, at whase retourning there was a grait concurs of the haill town, wha met him at the Nather Bow; and, going upe the streit, with bear heads and loud voices, sang to the prais of God, and testifeing of grait joy and consolation, the 124th Psalm, "Now Israel may say, and that trewlie," &c., till heavin and erthe resoundit. This noyes, when the Duc, being in the town, hard, and ludgit in the Hiegat, luiked out and saw, he raue his berde for anger, and hasted him af the town.'

Nine years later the tables were turned. James VI, who had consented to Durie's exile under Lennox's influence, after his escape from Bothwell's attempt on his life, went to 'the Great Kirk of Edinburgh' on December 28, 1591. Patrick Galloway preached the sermon 'and declared the King was come to give publict thanks to God for the same', and the 124th Psalm was sung.

Still another incident may be mentioned. When the two great branches of the divided Church of Scotland were united in October 1929, as the two processions marched, one upwards from the Mound, the other downwards by the Lawnmarket, to meet and coalesce at the top of Bank Street, on their way to St. Giles', the watching crowds who lined the streets spontaneously broke into singing, chiefly of Psalm cxxxiii, 'Behold, how good a thing it is', and of Psalm cxxiv.

ORLINGTON was for many years the fixed tune to the 23rd Psalm in some parts of Scotland. It appeared in 1854 in *The Sacred Psaltery, in four vocal parts, consisting principally of Original Psalm and Hymn Tunes*, the editor of which was John Campbell (q.v.). Its kinship with WILTSHIRE is obvious.

PALESTRINA is usually stated to be an adaptation from the *Gloria Patri* of the *Magnificat Tertii Toni* in Palestrina's *Magnificat Octo Tonorum* (1591). W. H. Monk's tune VICTORY, to 'The strife is o'er, the battle done', is derived from the same source, but, like this one, *longo intervallo*—at so long an interval indeed that it is no more than the initiatory suggestion that can be ascribed to Palestrina. See the note in this Supplement on the tune VICTORY, Hymn 122.

The present tune seems to have been published first in *The Parish Choir* in 1851, but in a metre of six lines of eight syllables each. The Common Metre form of it was made by T. L. Hately (q.v.), who published it in *The Church of Scotland Hymn Tune Book* of 1862, of which he was the musical editor.

PETERBOROUGH was composed by Sir John Goss in 1864, and published in the same year in *The Church Psalter and Hymn Book*, edited by the Rev. William Mercer (q.v. in *Handbook*). In the first *Church Hymnary* it was set to 'The spacious firmament on high'.

PHILIPPI was composed in 1835 by Samuel Wesley for *The Psalmist, a Collection of Psalm and Hymn Tunes*.

POTSDAM is an adaptation from the subject of the *Fugue in E* in Bach's *Forty-eight Preludes and Fugues*.

Dr. Greenhouse Allt, of St. Giles', Edinburgh, permits this interesting quotation from a work of his on 'the typical rhythm of the "Canzon alla francesce" :

'So Gabrieli, "Canzon ariosa" (1596). Froberger transforms it thus:

while Kerl (*c.* 1625–90), "Canzona V", thus

produces, as is well known, the composition adapted by Handel in *Israel in Egypt* as "Egypt was glad when they departed". In the major it is, of course, one of the oldest themes in the world, and finds its apotheosis in Bach's *Wohltemperirte Klavier* in the fugue (vol. ii, No. xxxiii) called by Samuel Wesley "The Saints in Glory",

PRAGUE appeared in *The Hymn Tunes of the Church of the Brethren. . . . Arranged for Four Voices in Score, by John Lees* (1824). Nearly all the tunes in this Moravian book are German chorales or derivatives from chorales. L. R. West was a minister of that Church, and the name given to this tune suggests that it also may have had a German origin.

ST. ANDREW appeared in *The New Harmony of Sion . . . by W. Tans'ur. Book II* (1764), where it is set to Psalm cl, and headed 'Barby Tune, composed in four parts, W.T.' The initials may mean no more than that the harmony was by Tans'ur.

ST. GEORGE appeared in *Ein Christlicher Abentreien, vom Leben und ampt Johannis des Tauffers . . . N.H. 1554*. This was a tract of seven leaves. Herman was a poet as well as a composer, and here he set the tune to a hymn of his own, 'Kommt her ihr liebsten Schwesterlein'. The melody is as follows:

In his collection of hymns entitled *Die Sontags Evangelia uber das gantze Jar, in Gesenge verfasset* (1560), he set the tune to his hymn 'Lobt Gott, ihr Christen, allzugleich', and with that hymn it has remained associated in Germany ever since. It has undergone various modifications both in German and English books. Bach gives it in four different forms in his arrangements of the Chorales.

See especially his treatment of it in Cantata 151, *Süsser Trost, mein Jesus kommt*, and the Wedding Cantata, *Dem Gerechten muss das Licht*.

ST. GEORGE'S, EDINBURGH appeared in *Sacred Harmony, for the use of St. George's Church, Edinburgh* (1820), which was prepared by Dr. Andrew Thomson (q.v.), minister of the church, with the assistance of R. A. Smith, who had not yet at that time become, as he did three years later, precentor of St. George's. The tune is inseparably associated in Scotland with Psalm xxiv, vv. 7–10. This psalm was customarily sung at Communion in many places in Scotland, while minister and elders were bringing the elements into the church in solemn procession before the administration of the ordinance began; and it was for this stately ceremonial act, which corresponds to the Great Entrance in the Eastern rite, that Dr. Thomson composed the tune. When the 35th Paraphrase came into use and displaced the psalm at this point, the custom arose of using the psalm as the first act of worship in the post-Communion service, a much less appropriate place for it.

ST. GREGORY is from *A Collection of Psalm Tunes interspersed with Airs, . . . set for four voices, for the use of Choirs and Families . . . and dedicated to S. Webbe, sen., by his son, S. Webbe, jun.* (1808). Webbe was at that time organist of a Unitarian church in Liverpool. Wainwright, who composed it, had died there twenty-six years before. The tune therefore is likely to have been known locally, and may have been printed in some ephemeral form, before Webbe published it.

It appeared also in *Euphonia, containing Sixty-two Psalm and Hymn Tunes . . . Harmonised, Arranged and Composed . . . by W. Dixon*. This book is undated, but it must have been published between 1805 and 1808.

ST. MIRREN is from *Sacred Music . . . sung in St. George's Church, Edinburgh, edited by R. A. Smith* (1825), the source from which 'Invocation' and 'Selma' were also derived. The name was given in homage to Paisley, Smith's father having been a Paisley weaver, and he himself precentor in the Abbey Church, 1807–23. Mirren here is not, as generally supposed, the Scots phonetic spelling of the name Marion, but the name of the Celtic saint Mirin, or Mirinus, a pupil of St. Comgall, abbot of Bangor, and a contemporary of St. Columba, whom he must have known, and of Columbanus. Leaving Ireland in 580, he became a missionary in the west and south-west of Scotland; his name lingers in Ayrshire, Dumbarton, and the Stewartry of Kirkcudbright, and it is a household word in Paisley, where, 'full of miracles and holiness, he slept in the Lord'. When the monks from Wenloc came to Paisley 600 years after his death, they found his memory green. In their charters and the bulls of the Popes they called him 'the glorious confessor St. Mirin'.

ST. NEOT appeared as WORKSOP TUNE in *A Collection of Choice Psalm-Tunes in Three and Four Parts; with New and Easie Psalm-Tunes, Hymns, Anthems, and Spiritual Songs. . . . Third edition, 1715.* This was edited by John and James Green. No trace can be found of the first two editions of the book. James Green was an organist in Hull in 1724, when he published, under his own name only, the fifth edition, the earliest known, of *A Book of Psalmody, containing Chanting Tunes, with eighteen Anthems, and Variety of Psalm-Tunes in Four Parts.*

The tune, under the name WORKSOP, is found in many collections of the eighteenth century. Green gives the melody in this form:

ST. NICHOLAS is from *The Spiritual Man's Companion: Or, The Pious Christian's Recreation. Containing . . . a Set of Psalm-Tunes, in One, Two, Three, and Four Parts, as they are sung in England and Scotland, &c. The Fifth Edition, with large Additions, never before Printed, by Israel Holdroyd, Philo-Musicae* (1753). The tune is there set to Psalm cxix, Second Part, Old Version, and headed ST. NICHOLAS'S TUNE. No composer's name is given. The form of the melody is this:

In Riley's *Parochial Music Corrected* (1762) it is given thus:

Later books exhibit various slight differences in the form of the melody, especially in the close of line 1 and in line 4. The earliest appearance of the tune in Scotland appears to have been in *The Rudiments of Music: To which is added, A Collection of the best Church Tunes, Hymns, Canons, and Anthems. By James Thomson, Philo-Musicae* (Edinburgh, 1778). The present form, so far as can be traced, appeared first in *Scottish Psalmody*, 1854, where it is said to have been 'arranged by Herr Dürrner'.

ST. SEPULCHRE appeared first in *The Congregational Hymn and Tune Book*, edited by the Rev. R. R. Chope (1862), where it was set to the hymn 'Lord Jesu! when we stand afar'. It had been composed, however, in 1836, when the composer's father was organist of St. Sepulchre's Church, London. Cooper himself became organist there seven years later. The tune is sometimes known as 'St. Agnes'.

ST. THOMAS (C.M.) is from *A Collection of Tunes suited to the several Metres commonly used in Public Worship, set in Four Parts ... by C. Ashworth*. This book is undated, but it must have been published about 1760, as the third edition, printed from the same plates, is dated 1766. In both the name given is 'Walney Tune'. The form of it is as follows:

Its first appearance in Scotland, so far as is known, was in Thomas Moore's *The Psalm Singer's Delightful Companion* (Glasgow, 1762), where it is in the present form and bears its present name.

In some old collections it is ascribed to Purcell, but such random and groundless ascriptions were then common, HANOVER, for instance, being attributed to Handel, ST. STEPHEN to Battishill, WALTON, under the horrific name of 'Necropolis', to Beethoven, J. F. Lampe's KENT to Green, and not ST. THOMAS only, but STROUD-WATER, WALSALL, and BURFORD to Purcell.

ST. THOMAS (S.M.) appeared in *The New Universal Psalmodist* published by Aaron Williams in 1770, where it is named ST. THOMAS'S and set to Psalm xlviii, 'Great is the Lord our God'. Williams (1731–76) was a music engraver and publisher, a teacher of music also, and clerk (leader of praise) in the Scots Church, London Wall. He published a number of important collections of psalmody. The one named had a great popularity, for the first edition appeared in 1763, and the fourth and fifth (from the latter the present tune was taken) in 1770. In the fourth edition another tune also called

'St. Thomas's' appears, which bears no resemblance to this one. In the original form of the present tune the second line begins thus:

and the third ends:

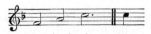

SERENITY appeared in Cornelius Bryan's *A Collection of the most esteemed Psalm Tunes, Ancient and Modern, Selected and Harmonised for Four Voices, and interspersed with a few original Compositions* (*c.* 1830). No name is there given to it. The second line had this difference:

SHEFFIELD appeared first in William Mather's *Sacred Music, consisting of Twenty-six Psalm and Hymn Tunes . . . composed in an Easy Style for the Children of Charity Schools, by William Mather, Organist of St. Paul's and St. James's Churches, Sheffield, &c.* This book bears no date, but it must have appeared about 1800, for the tune appears also in *Dr. Watts's Psalms and Hymns, set to new music . . . composed by Edward Miller . . . to which is added a copious Appendix containing the most favourite tunes now used in different Congregations* (1802). Curiously, in the latter book it is marked in the index as a 'new tune, never before printed'. Mather called it 'Lively', and set it to Psalm xxiii, 'My Shepherd is the living Lord'. Miller (the famous Doncaster organist who adapted TUNBRIDGE as ROCKINGHAM) named it SHEFFIELD and set it to Mrs. Elizabeth Rowe's hymn, 'Begin the high celestial strain'.

SOLOMON is adapted from the solo 'What though I trace each herb and flower' in Handel's oratorio *Solomon*, composed in 1748. In the form in which the tune is usually given the first strain is closely similar to that of TALLIS. In the present arrangement this likeness is minimized by reversion to Handel's original, which is as follows:

The rest follows the original, note for note, and as much of the accompaniment as could be incorporated has been retained.

STOCKTON was originally named 'Elizabeth', but was given its present name while still in manuscript. It was sung in the parish churches of Stockton and Wakefield, and was popular in both, for years before it was published. The change of name took place about 1820, but there was no publication until the tune was included in *Hymns Ancient and Modern* (1861), with alterations by Dr. J. B. Dykes, which were not improvements, thus:

The present form reverts to Wright's original.

STROUDWATER, named from the river on which Stroud stands in Gloucestershire, appeared in *A Book of Psalmody, containing some easy instructions for young beginners; to which is added a select number of Psalm-tunes, Hymns, and Anthems. Collected, Printed, Taught, and Sold by Matthew Wilkins of Great Milton, near Thame in Oxfordshire* (c. 1730). Wilkins was a butcher at Great Milton, and evidently a musical enthusiast. His book went into at least a second edition (c. 1735). He names the tune 'Stroudwater New Tune' to distinguish it from a 'Stroudwater Old Tune', entirely different, which also he includes. The former was set to Psalm cxlvi, the latter to Psalm xl. The third line has a slight difference from the familiar form:

The tune has evidently become disused in the country of its origin, for the musical editor of *Songs of Praise Discussed* (1933) says of it, 'It is an excellent tune, and should rapidly become popular'.

UXBRIDGE is from *The Standard Psalm Tune Book . . . Arranged for 4 voices with an organ accompaniment, by Henry Edward Dibdin* [q.v.] . . . (1851). According to the loose habit which then prevailed of ascribing tunes to distinguished composers without any proof that the ascription was justified, Dibdin headed this tune 'Ascribed to Purcell'. His book is 'notoriously untrustworthy as regards the source and authorship of tunes'; but most books of the period stand in the same condemnation.

WILTSHIRE was long better known in Scotland as 'New St. Ann', and doubtless it was this that led to its being for a time currently ascribed to Dr. Croft. It appeared in *Divine Amusement: Being a Selection of the most admired Psalms, Hymns, and Anthems used at St. James's Chapel . . .* (c. 1795). Smart was at that time organist of the chapel. He set the tune to Psalm xlviii. The original form is given with a figured bass, as below, and there is a note at the beginning of the volume to this effect: 'For the accommodation of those who do not understand Thorough Bass, it is explained in Small Notes, which may be Played or Omitted at Pleasure.' Observe how a misreading of these small notes led to a modification of the tune at the beginning of the second line.

From this it will be seen that at the beginning of the second line the small notes have been incorporated into the tune, and the notes of the original melody have been transferred to the alto part. This change was sanctioned by the composer, for he himself adopted it when he included the tune in his own *Collection of Sacred Music* in 1863; he also gave his approval to the present form when it was included by Dr. Andrew Henderson of Paisley in his *Church Melodies* in 1856. The tune has been subjected to many changes in different collections.

WITTENBERG, also known as 'Reading' and as 'Spires', is also, in some of the old tune-books, called '*Serva nos, Domine*', from the Latin of the first words of Luther's hymn, 'Erhalt uns, Herr, bei deinem Wort', to which the tune was originally set in Klug's *Gesangbuch* (1543). A close translation of it by Robert Wisdome used to be printed at the end of the Old (English) Version of the Psalms. The first verse ran thus:

> Preserve us, Lord, by Thy deare word;
> From Turk and Pope defend us, Lord,
> Both which would thrust out of His throne
> Our Lord Christ Jesus, Thy dear Son.

In Klug the hymn is headed in characteristic fashion, 'A children's Song, to be sung against the two Arch-enemies of Christ and His holy Church, the Pope and the Turk.' Hence the tune came to be known as 'the Pope and Turk tune', popular opinion having apparently decided that the Pope was the worse enemy of the two! It is printed by Klug in the old notation, and is believed to be based on a plainsong melody. In several versions the second last note is sharp, but it is natural in the original, and this gives support to the belief that originally the tune was plainsong.

Hymn and tune were exceedingly popular in England. In the older collections they were never omitted, and they continued to appear in most till the close of the eighteenth century; they appeared as late as 1832 (in J. Bickersteth's *Psalms and Hymns*).

In *Daye's Psalter* (1563) the tune appears both in its simple form and with an elaborate harmonization. Two earlier settings (1563 and 1592) may be seen in the Historical Edition of *Hymns Ancient and Modern* (1904).

YORK was one of the twelve Common Tunes in *The CL Psalmes of David, in Prose and Meeter, with their whole Usuall Tunes*, published by Andro Hart in Edinburgh in 1615. It is there named 'The Stilt', doubtless because the somewhat awkward movement of the first and third phrases suggests the swinging difficult gait of a man walking on stilts. 'St. David' is another Stilt. Robert Bridges says: 'The best stilts are beautiful, and together with their active vigour they show an unexpected plaintiveness in fetching their long intervals.'

These Common Tunes were a new departure in Scottish psalmody. Till then each psalm was given its 'proper' tune; but a concession had to be made to the average person's difficulty in mastering many tunes, and this was done by introducing Common Tunes without any special psalm being specified to be sung to them, so that they might be used for any psalm versified in common metre.

In Ravenscroft's *Whole Book of Psalms* (1621) the tune appears four times, with three different harmonizations, two of them by John Milton, father of the poet. One of these is the arrangement used in the present Psalter. This association of the name Milton with the tune led many compilers to assume that the poet composed it; thus in many old collections it is definitely assigned to him. No countenance to such an idea is given by Ravenscroft, who classes it as a 'Northern Tune', and 'proper for joyful ditties'! It was he who abandoned the Scots name and called it 'Yorke'.

For a long time, next to OLD 100TH, it was the most popular tune in England; in some places, at the time of the decadence, it was almost the only tune known. So late as 1762 a writer says that he has heard YORK sung fifteen times in one week in the same church. Sir John Hawkins says that it was sung as a lullaby by 'half the nurses in England', and he adds, 'the chimes of many country churches have played it six or eight times in four-and-twenty hours from time immemorial.' In Scotland it had an equal favour. When the number of tunes in use there sank to twelve, and in the Highlands to five, YORK was one of the number retained in use.

It is possible that the tune may have originated in a church chime. The first and third strains, which are identical, suggest a 'change' in a six-bell chime; they are in fact part of a tune known in Cornwall as 'Stratton Church Chimes'. This tune was contributed to *English County Songs*, edited by L. E. Broadwood and J. A. Fuller-Maitland (1893), together with old rhymes locally sung to it, one being:

> They bored a hole in Oliver's nose
> And put therein a ring,
> And drew him round about the town
> For murdering Charles our king.

There is some evidence for believing that this rhyme from the days of Cavaliers and Roundheads is a late edition of an earlier one in which the Jew is the 'guy' exhibited as an object of hatred.

The Stratton tune, given below, does not appear to have been founded on YORK as we know it, because on the same chimes YORK itself could have been played except for one note—the raised fourth which marks the modulation to the dominant at the end of the second strain, for which another could easily have been substituted. (Did Hawkins hear this sharpened note on the country church chimes of which he speaks?) The same six-bell chime would seem also to have belonged to Osney Abbey, Oxfordshire, long ago destroyed, for 'The Bells of Osney' is the alternative name for 'Turn again, Whittington', which is composed on the same six notes of the scale. The bells of Osney were famous in olden times.

As for YORK's earlier name 'The Stilt', the tendency of most church choirs to accent the higher notes of the tune, which fall on the second and fourth beats of its natural rhythm, accounts for most of its awkwardness. If it were written in $\frac{4}{4}$ time, with the natural accent on the first and third beats only—as in the verse set to Stratton chimes—its 'stilted' character would disappear. It would benefit at the same time by fewer changes of harmony, so that, as 'proper for joyful ditties', it could be sung less slowly and more rhythmically, like the joyful chiming of bells.

BIOGRAPHICAL NOTES

ADDITIONS AND CORRECTIONS

ABÉLARD, Pierre. In line 5 of the *Handbook* note 'buried by Héloïse' should read 'buried beside Héloïse'.

ALCOCK, Walter Galpin, Mus.Doc., b. 1861, was knighted, 1933.

ALDRICH, Henry, D.D. (Westminster, 1647–1710, Oxford), was one of the most remarkable figures in academic England in his time. Educated at Westminster School and Christ Church, Oxford, he became rector of Wem, Shropshire; tutor in Christ Church, canon in 1681, Dean in 1689; Vice-Chancellor of the University, 1692–5. He was the first amateur of his day. 'Divinity, classics, architecture, logic, polemics, and music engaged his attention in turn, and in all he did well.' His *Artis Logicae Rudimenta* was used as a text-book at Oxford till within living memory. The monuments of his architectural ability, in three sides of Peckwater Quadrangle in Christ Church, the Chapel of Trinity College, and All Saints' Church, High Street, Oxford, suggest that the admiration it evoked was aroused less by the merit of his achievement than by wonderment that a man skilled in so many other things could in an art remote from his other interests do so well. He was one of the first members of the Philosophical Society, the forerunner of the Royal Society, and was active in Church affairs, acting for a time as Prolocutor of Canterbury Convocation. In music he showed no originality, but a skill remarkable in a man so many-sided. He is best known by his *Smoaking Catch* (he was himself an inveterate smoker), so arranged that the four men singing it are given time to take puffs at the rests provided for the purpose. Of this catch and another—*Hark, the bonny Christ Church Bells*—Henry Davey says that they are the only two catches of the Restoration period endurable at the present day. Another, long well known, was *Great Tom is cast*. The Dean wrote many anthems, and his *Service in G* is still heard in cathedrals. He was an attractive personality. 'The suavity of his manners, the hilarity of his conversation, the variety and excellence of his talents, in conjunction with a fine person, conciliated and attached all committed to his superintendence, to such a degree that his last surviving disciples of the first rank have been unable to speak recollectedly of their intercourse with him, without the tenderest indications of affection to his memory.'

98. CHANT IN A.

Biographical Notes

ARMITAGE, ELLA SOPHIA (d. 1931, Middlesbrough), was one of the five original students of Miss Clough at the beginning of Newnham College. She had an intimate knowledge of seven languages, in addition to a fair acquaintance with classical and New Testament Greek. Principal Griffith Jones of Bradford says of her that she was 'a personality of rich gifts and rare attainments; of beautiful piety; sympathetic, generously kind, and nobly hospitable. . . . She always reminded me of what Henry Ward Beecher said of his Aunt Esther, that "she was a woman so beautiful in spirit and so modest in temper that when she went to heaven she would spend ages wondering how she got there, and the angels would be wondering how it was that she had not been there from all eternity".'

ARNOLD, SAMUEL, Mus.Doc. (London, 1740–1802, Westminster), was educated at the Chapel Royal under Bernard Gates and Nares. In 1763 he was appointed composer to Covent Garden Theatre. In 1769 he became owner of Marylebone Gardens, where he produced burlettas, operas, and entertainments of a dramatic kind, two of which were written by Chatterton. The speculation was financially a failure; before he withdrew he had lost £10,000. Oxford gave him his Mus.Doc. degree in 1773. In 1783 he succeeded Nares as organist and composer to the Chapel Royal; in 1784 was sub-director of the Handel Commemoration; from 1789 was conductor of the Academy of Ancient Music; and in 1798 became organist of Westminster Abbey. He wrote many songs for Vauxhall Gardens, glees, forty-three operas, after-pieces, and burlettas or pantomimes, many of which contained melodies which should not be allowed to die, four oratorios, and many anthems. He also edited *Cathedral Music* in four volumes, a continuation of Boyce; *Psalms of David for Parish Churches* (along with J. W. Callcott); and *The Works of Handel* in thirty-six volumes, at the request of George III; this last he was unable to complete because of want of patronage. His epitaph in the Abbey is as follows:

> Here lies of genius, probity, and worth
> All that belongs to nature and to earth.
> The hand that freely felt and warmly gave,
> The heart that pity stretched to help and save,
> The form that late a glowing spirit warmed,
> Whose science tutor'd and whose talents charmed,
> Whose spirit fled to Him who spirit gave,
> Now smiles triumphant o'er the feeble grave
> That could not chain it here, and joins to raise
> With Heaven's own choir the song of prayer and praise.
> Oh Shade revered! Our nation's loss and pride,
> For mute was harmony when ARNOLD died.

25. ARNOLD.   23. CHANT IN B♭.

79. LANGHOLM.

Biographical Notes

AYLWARD, Theodore (?, 1730–1801, London), was organist of Oxford Chapel, London, *c.* 1760; St. Lawrence Jewry, 1762; St. Michael, Cornhill, 1768; in 1769 received the prize medal from the Catch Club for his glee *A Cruel Fate*; in 1771 became Professor of Music in Gresham College; and in 1788 organist and master of the choristers, St. George's Chapel, Windsor; he was also private organist to Queen Charlotte. He composed glees, songs, and musical dramas. On his tombstone in St. George's this epitaph, by Hayley, is engraved:

> Aylward, adieu! my pleasing gentle friend,
> Regret and honour on thy grave attend.
> Thy rapid hand harmonious skill possest,
> And moral harmony enriched thy breast,
> For heaven most freely to thy life assign'd
> Benevolence, the music of the mind;
> Mild as thy nature all thy mortal scene,
> Thy death was easy, and thy life serene.

119–113. CHANT IN D♭.

BATHURST, William Henry. To his publications add *The Roman Antiquities of Lydney Park* (pub. posthumously, 1879).

BAXTER, Richard. Probably few nowadays would be inclined to take Johnson's heroic and incautious advice to Boswell: 'I asked him what works of Richard Baxter's I should read. He said, "Read any of them; they are all good."' There is humour now in this recommendation, for the standard edition of Baxter's *Practical Works* is in no fewer than twenty-three large octavo volumes.

BEETHOVEN, Ludwig van (Bonn, 1770–1827, Vienna), was of Flemish ancestry, but was himself wholly German, son and grandson of musicians at the court of the Elector of Cologne. His childhood was extremely unhappy. At 8 he played at a concert, and at 12 published nine variations on a march by Dressler. In 1784 he became second court organist; in 1785 composed three piano and string quartets; in 1787 visited Vienna and met Mozart; in 1792 met Haydn at Bonn and dedicated a cantata to him. When he settled in Vienna in 1792 he was already one of the finest pianoforte players of the day. His first pianoforte concerto was published in 1795. In 1798 he began to grow deaf, and the deafness grew until in 1822 he had to be turned round, when conducting, to realize that the audience was applauding; for the last few years he could not conduct conversations except in writing. He was slow to publish, but when he began, the eight years ending with 1802 saw the production of 92 compositions, including his only oratorio *The Mount of Olives* and two symphonies. He was a prodigious worker, and took endless pains with what he wrote: there is scarcely a bar of

97   H

his music of which it may not be said that it was re-written a dozen times. His brain teemed with ideas. His sketch-books were crammed with notes for symphonies. If he had carried out all the symphonies he had begun, there would have been fifty more. He was a mighty genius. This was recognized in his lifetime, and he was appreciated and honoured. His name will always be associated with the symphony; his nine symphonies are his greatest as well as his most representative works.

43. CONSOLATION.

BEXFIELD, WILLIAM RICHARD, Mus.Doc. (Norwich, 1824–53, London), was trained under Dr. Buck in Norwich Cathedral. As a boy he had a voice of remarkable sweetness and sang with rare charm. He became organist at Boston, Lincolnshire, in 1846, and two years later, of St. Helen's, Bishopsgate, London, the parish in which Byrd, Wilbye, Sir Thomas Gresham, and other notable musicians had lived. In 1848 he received from Oxford the Mus. Doc. degree. He wrote an oratorio, *Israel Restored*, which was performed in 1851 at the Norwich Musical Festival.

137 (2). CHANT IN c♯.

BLUNT, FREDERIC WILLIAM (Mayfair, London, 1839–1921, London), was educated at East Sheen, London, and at Rugby; was articled to his father as a solicitor and practised as such in London till he retired in 1918; was fond of music and sang a great deal in his younger days. He is believed to have written only one other tune, now lost. LYNDHURST appeared anonymously in *Church Praise*, first edition, 1882.

BOOTH, JOSIAH, d. London, 1930.

BORTHWICK, JANE LAURIE. Add to hymn under this name: 602. 'Still on the homeward journey'.

BOYD, WILLIAM, d. London, 1928. For some time before his death he was blind. While he was vicar of All Saints, Norfolk Square, he had three organists who were destined to reach high eminence—E. C. Bairstow, Hamilton Harty, and William Wolstenholme.

BRIDGES, ROBERT (SEYMOUR), d. Boar's Hill, Oxford, 1930.

BROOMFIELD, WILLIAM ROBERT. The statement in the *Handbook* that Broomfield was buried in a corner of the poorhouse grounds is inaccurate. His funeral took place on Friday, October 19, 1888, from the Hospital of St. Nicholas Poorhouse to St. Peter's Cemetery, Aberdeen. Before the coffin was taken out of the room the party of mourners sang part of Psalm li to his tune ST. KILDA.

BROWNE, SIMON (d. 1732), wrote the exposition of 1 Corinthians in Matthew Henry's *Commentary*. The inscription on the tablet to his memory in Shepton Mallet Unitarian Chapel is as follows: 'Near this Place lies the Remains / of Mr. Simon Browne, Minister of / the Gospel A Native of this Town / but known throughout the Nation by his Writings / Portsmouth and London enjoyed his / Ministry And when Nature was op/prest with so strange a Disorder that / He thought himself less than man / he attacked the boldest Infidels of the / age and tryumphed in the cause of / God. He dy'd A.D. 1732. Aet. 52.'

BRYAN, CORNELIUS (Bristol, *c*. 1775–1840, Bristol), was organist of St. Mark's (the Mayor's) Chapel, Bristol; later, also of St. Mary Redcliffe, holding both appointments at the same time. While conducting an operetta *Lundy*, of his own composition, in the Theatre Royal, Bristol, he fell through a trapdoor which had not been properly fastened, and so injured his spine that he died a few days later. About 1840 he published *A Collection of the most esteemed Psalm Tunes, Ancient and Modern, Selected and Harmonised for Four Voices, and interspersed with a few original Compositions*; he published also some organ pieces.

174. SERENITY.

BUCK, PERCY CARTER, Mus.Doc., was Musical Director of Harrow School, 1901–27, and is now Musical Adviser to the London County Council.

BUNNETT, EDWARD, Mus.Doc. Norfolk Cathedral should, of course, be Norwich.

BYRD, WILLIAM (b. 1543), became a cathedral organist, at Lincoln, at the age of twenty. It was in 1570 that he became a member of the Chapel Royal. About 1593 he became a country gentleman at Stondon Place, Essex, and during the latter part of his life realized his ambition of founding a county family. Tallis and he, in gratitude for the privilege given them by the Queen, dedicated to her their joint work, *Cantiones Sacrae*. His contemporaries had no doubt about his greatness; 'a Father of Musicke' was a title they more than once bestowed on him, and one calls him 'ye inimitable'. He wrote excellent Latin, was a man of sound sense and excellent culture, and exercised an enormous influence in his lifetime. He was the father of the madrigalists and the virginal composers, and by far the greatest musical pioneer this country has ever known. His birth-year is variously given, but as his will in 1622 states that he was then in his 80th year, 1543 is taken to be correct.

BYRNE, MARY ELIZABETH (Dublin, 1881–1931, Dublin), was educated at the Dominican Convent in Eccles Street, Dublin. At the Royal University she graduated as M.A. with first-class honours in Modern Literature, and gained a studentship. For some years she worked at the Catalogue of the Royal Irish Academy, the 3rd fasciculus of which (1928) was compiled by her. An edition of *Tain Bo Fraich*, largely her work, is soon to appear. Her chief employment was on the *Dictionary of the Irish Language*, but her part of the work is not yet (1935) published.

BYROM, JOHN, was in every way a remarkable man. 'Extremely tall, he wore a peculiar slouched hat, from under which peered a face at once benignant and inquisitive.' He was the chief inventor of modern shorthand (his *Universal English Shorthand* was published in 1767); and it was owing to his having taught the Wesleys this form of rapid writing that Charles was able to dash his hymns down in shorthand as they came into his mind. He was made an F.R.S. in 1724.

He was a wit; some of his epigrams are not likely to be forgotten. When the Pretender marched into England in the '45, Byrom came out on his side, but afterwards covered himself by the famous lines (cf. *Redgauntlet*, ch. vii):

> God bless the King!—I mean the Faith's Defender!
> God bless—no harm in blessing—the Pretender:
> Who that Pretender is, and who that King,
> God bless us all!—is quite another thing.

He was also the inventor of Tweedledum and Tweedledee, in connexion with the extraordinary rivalry of Bononcini and Handel (1726–34), and the operatic war between them which rent society into opposing factions, was fomented by a copious flow of scurrilous pamphlets and poems, and was even taken up by the two political parties. It was when Handel revived his English Pastoral, with additions from his early Italian work, *Aci, Galatea e Polifemo*, and Bononcini produced a rival serenata, that Byrom wrote:

> Some say, compar'd to Bononcini,
> That Mynheer Handel's but a ninny;
> Others aver that he to Handel
> Is scarcely fit to hold a candle.
> Strange all this difference should be
> 'Twixt Tweedledum and Tweedledee.

Byrom was withal a man of rare piety. F. T. Palgrave, in *The Treasury of Sacred Song* (p. 349), says of him that he was 'one of the many men of strong feeling in whom faith burned "like a hidden flame" through the eighteenth century'.

CAMIDGE, JOHN, Mus.Doc. (York, 1790–1859, York), son of Matthew Camidge (q.v.) and grandson of John the elder, took his Mus.Doc. degree in 1829, and was appointed organist of York

Minster in 1842, after performing the duties for many years on behalf of his father. In 1848, while playing the evening service, he was stricken with paralysis, and never played again. His duties were then taken by his son, Thomas Simpson Camidge. In 1828 he published a volume of cathedral music of his own composition.

The record of the Camidge family in music was remarkable. At the farewell service for the Rt. Rev. Charles E. Camidge, D.D., after his consecration as Bishop of Bathurst, in York Minster in October, 1887, the music included compositions by five generations of the Camidge family, relatives of the Bishop. These were—John the first, Matthew, John the second, Dr. T. S. Camidge, and his son, John the third, organist of Beverley Minster.

116. CHANT (D) IN E.

CAMIDGE, Matthew (York, 1758–1844, York), son of John the elder, was educated at the Chapel Royal under Dr. Nares, returned to York as assistant to his father, and in 1799 succeeded him as organist of the Minster. He resigned in 1842. He published sonatas, marches for the pianoforte, a collection of *Tunes adapted to Sandys's Version of the Psalms* (York, 1789), and *A Method of Instruction in Music, by Questions and Answers.*

22–23. CHANT (D) IN E.

22–1, 51. CHANT (D) IN e.

CAMPBELL, John (Paisley, 1807–60, Glasgow), a merchant in Glasgow, was an amateur in music and an organist. He was one of the first members of Glasgow Choral Union. 'He had the misfortune to flourish at a time when our psalmody was sadly blemished by florid divisions and repeating lines, and naturally he followed the same bad pattern in most of his tunes.' He published: *The Sacred Psaltery in four vocal parts, consisting principally of original psalm and hymn tunes* (Glasgow, 1854)—nearly fifty tunes, and his anthem *Rejoice in the Lord*, which was long popular in the West of Scotland. He edited also *Campbell's Selection of Anthems and Doxologies, with a separate piano accompaniment* (Glasgow, 1848); also Hamilton's collection of *Anthems, Choruses, Sanctuses,* &c., with another anthem, *I will sing of the mercies of the Lord*, six anthems by R. A. Smith, and several of Handel's choruses.

93. ORLINGTON.

CAREY, Henry. The story about his birth is described by Sir John Squire as an exploded myth.

CHIPP, Edmund Thomas (London, 1823–86, Nice), son of T. P. Chipp, well known as the player of the 'Tower Drums', was one of Dr. William Hawes' choristers at the Chapel Royal. As a violinist he was a member of the Queen's private band and of other orchestras.

As organist he held office in Albany Chapel, Regent's Park, 1843–6; St. Mary-at-Hill, Eastcheap, 1852; the Royal Panopticon, Leicester Square, in succession to W. T. Best, 1855; Holy Trinity, Paddington, 1856; St. George's Church and the Ulster Hall, Belfast, 1862; Kinnaird Hall, Dundee, and St. Paul's Episcopal Church, Edinburgh, 1866; and in the same year organist and magister choristarum, Ely Cathedral. He took his Mus.Doc. degree at Cambridge in 1860. His works included an oratorio, *Job*; *Naomi, a Sacred Idyl*; and much church music.

6. CHANT IN f.

COCKBURN, ROBERT WILLIAM, LL.B., W.S. (Edinburgh, 1879–), was educated at Merchiston Castle School and the University, Edinburgh; at the latter he took the degrees of M.A. and LL.B. Since 1904 he has practised as a Writer to the Signet. He has always been interested as an amateur in the theory and practice of music, and since boyhood has deputized for over seventy church organists. He has been an elder in North Morningside Church, Edinburgh, since 1917, and is also Preses of the congregation. He is a member of the Committee on Public Worship and Aids to Devotion of the Church of Scotland, and was one of the revisers of the music of the Scottish Psalter, 1928–9.

13. Appendix 13. OLD 100TH.
Arrangements of 38, 128, and 182.

CONDER, JOSIAH, married a grand-daughter of Roubiliac, the famous sculptor, and the hereditary geographical, literary, and artistic ability of the family was seen in two of their grandsons, Colonel Claude R. Conder, R.E., author, archaeologist, and surveyor of Palestine, and Charles Conder, the well-known artist.

COOKE, BENJAMIN, Mus.Doc. (London, 1734–93, Westminster), became in his ninth year a pupil of Dr. Pepusch, and in three years' time was able to take the place of John Robinson at the organ in Westminster Abbey. In 1752 he succeeded Pepusch as conductor of the Academy of Ancient Music, and in 1757 became master of the choristers, Westminster Abbey; in 1757 lay vicar there; in 1762 organist in succession to Robinson; and in 1782 organist also of St. Martin's-in-the-Fields. He had the Mus.Doc. degree from both Cambridge and Oxford. His fine Service in G was composed for the reopening of the Abbey organ. He composed much church music besides, anthems, chants, and psalm and hymn tunes; and in addition, many fine glees, canons, &c. A collection of his glees was published in his lifetime, and after his death a second collection appeared under the editorship of his son Robert. The epitaph on his tomb in the Abbey says: 'His professional knowledge, talents and skill were profound, pleasing, and various: in his works they are recorded, and within these walls their power has been felt and understood. The simplicity of his manners, the integrity of his heart, and the innocency of his life have numbered him among those who kept the commandments of God, and the faith of their Saviour Jesus Christ.' Then follows his AMEN, a masterly canon, three in one, by double augmentation, which he intended to be sung at the close of Byrd's 'Non nobis'.

73–*18*. CHANT (D) IN a.
32. CHANT (D) IN B♭.

COOPER, GEORGE (Lambeth, 1820–76, London), was son of the assistant organist at St. Paul's. At the age of eleven he deputized for his father. Attwood delighted in hearing him extemporize. Before he was fourteen he was organist of St. Benet, Paul's Wharf. He succeeded his father in the assistant organistship of St. Paul's; in 1836 became organist of St. Ann and St. Agnes; in 1843 followed his father at St. Sepulchre's and was singing-master and organist to Christ's Hospital as well; in 1856 was appointed organist of the Chapel Royal. 'It is as a performer on and arranger for the organ that he will be long remembered. . . . As a player of Bach he was simply unsurpassed.' He published an *Organist's Assistant*, a series of arrangements; an *Organist's Manual. . . . Select Movements from the most eminent composers*; part-songs, &c.

15. ST. SEPULCHRE.

CORFE, JOSEPH (Salisbury, 1740–1820, Salisbury), after training as a chorister in Salisbury Cathedral, became a gentleman of the Chapel Royal in 1783; sang in the Handel Commemoration in 1784; and was organist and master of the choristers in Salisbury from 1792 till 1804, when he resigned in favour of his son, Arthur Thomas Corfe. He died suddenly while kneeling in prayer at his bedside, and was buried in the Cathedral cloisters. He was author of a book on *Harmony and Thorough Bass*, and published a volume of cathedral music, containing a Morning and an Evening Service in B flat, and eleven anthems.

*8. CHANT (D) IN C.

COTTERILL, THOMAS. Lane End, Staffordshire, is now Longton.

CUMMINGS, WILLIAM HAYMAN, Mus.Doc. (Sidbury, Devon, 1831–1915, London), was trained as a chorister in St. Paul's and the Temple Church; sang as alto in the London performance of *Elijah*, 1847; became organist of Waltham Abbey, 1847; tenor singer in the Temple Church and Westminster Abbey; then a leading concert tenor, identified with the tenor parts in Bach's Passion music, &c.; professor of singing in the Royal College for the Blind, Norwood; also at the Royal Academy of Music, 1879–96; Principal of the Guildhall School of Music, 1896–1911. He was one of the founders of the Purcell Society and edited 3 volumes of its publications. His works included a cantata *The Fairy Ring*, a biographical dictionary, a *Primer of the Rudiments of Music*, and a Life of Purcell. He had a remarkable musical library, and was a keen musical antiquary.

46 (Hymnary). BETHLEHEM (adaptation).

CUMMINS, JOHN JAMES, went to London, not in 1864 but in 1834.

DARLING, THOMAS. Shanington should be Thanington.

DAVIES, Sir HENRY WALFORD, C.V.O., O.B.E., resigned the organistship of St. George's, Windsor, in 1932. He was appointed Master of the King's Musick, 1934, and in the same year was made a freeman of Oswestry, his native town. He was joint-editor of *The Church Anthem Book* (1933).

103. CHANT (D) IN C.

DECK, JAMES GEORGE (b. 1807), served the East India Company in the 14th Madras Native Infantry.

DIBDIN, HENRY EDWARD (Sadler's Wells, 1813–66, Edinburgh), grandson of Charles Dibdin, the composer of popular songs, was a clever harpist, and as such played at Covent Garden when Paganini made his last appearance there, in 1832. In the following year he went to Edinburgh, where he was organist of Trinity Chapel and became a teacher of music. Though he composed a few psalm tunes and pieces for organ and pianoforte, he is best known as compiler of *The Standard Psalm Tune Book*, described as 'the largest and most authentic collection of psalm tunes ever published, the contents being mainly derived from ancient psalters'; also of *The Praise Book* (1865). Dibdin had a somewhat uncritical mind: his attributions of tunes to composers are frequently ludicrously astray. See note on ST. PAUL in this Supplement.

*138. UXBRIDGE.

DIX, LEOPOLD L. The hymn-book to which he contributed his arrangements was *The Church Hymnal* of the Irish Episcopal Church, 1919.

DRAPER, WILLIAM HENRY, D.D., d. 1933.

DUNCALF, HENRY, was organist in 1752 of St. Bartholomew-the-Little-by-the-Exchange, a church destroyed in 1841, and at the same time of St. Mary-at-Hill, which still stands.

DYKES, JOHN BACCHUS. Lord Kelvin, in his later years, spoke of his debt to 'the incomparable John Dykes'. Dykes wrote tunes for all who applied to him, not grudgingly or of necessity, and frequently refused payment for them. The last tune he wrote was for *The Congregational Hymn Book*.

ELLIS, WILLIAM, Mus.Doc. (Cantuar.) 1929.

FALCONER, HUGH, D.D., d. Moffat, 1931.

FELTON, WILLIAM. His *Gavot* was often set to the words, 'Farewell, Manchester, noble town, farewell'. The inscription on the memorial tablet in the cloisters of Hereford Cathedral is as follows: 'Gul. Felton, A.M. / hujusque ecclesiae succentor / Collegii Vicariorum Choralium / Custos / Frederico Walliae Principi a sacris / vir animose justus / multiplici doctrina eruditus / Rerum musicarum peritissimus / Obiit sexto die Decembris A.D. MDCCLXIX. Aetatis LIV.'

> *42, 43.* CHANT IN E♭.
> *91.* CHANT IN G.

FINLAY, KENNETH GEORGE, in 1928 resolved to devote himself altogether to music, and after a year at the Royal College of Music and another at the Teachers' Training College, Jordanhill, Glasgow, was appointed in 1930 a teacher of class singing at Irvine, under the Ayrshire County Council. He has published papers dealing with Safety of Life at Sea in the *Transactions* of the Institute of Naval Architects; hymn-tunes in many collections, a cantata *The Saviour's Birth* (1928), and many unaccompanied choral works and educational part-songs.

FITZHERBERT, WILLIAM (?, 1713–97, St. Paul's College, London), was in 1744 elected to the fourth minor canonry, which carried with it the title of Epistolar, in St. Paul's Cathedral. In 1746 he was appointed one of the priests of the Chapel Royal, and in 1776 Sub-Dean of the Cathedral. From 1751 to 1778 he was a minor canon also of St. Peter's, Westminster. He became rector of Hadlow, Kent, in 1753; of Hornedon-on-the-Hill, Essex, in 1756. He held the latter cure till 1771, and then passed to St. Gregory by St. Paul, London. On his Double Chant in F, Dr. Crotch once composed a very clever fugue. The second half of the chant is believed not to be Fitzherbert's, but to have been added, not improbably by Dr. Philip Hayes (q.v.), 'who was somewhat fond of adding his own effusions to those of other people'.

> *50.* CHANT (D) IN F.

FLINTOFT, LUKE (Worcester, 1678–1727, London), graduated at Queens' College, Cambridge, in 1700, took holy orders, and became priest-vicar, Lincoln Cathedral, in 1704; passed to a similar office in Worcester Cathedral in 1714; became a gentleman of the Chapel Royal, 1715; reader in Whitehall Chapel, 1719; minor canon of Westminster Abbey, 1719. The chapter books of the Abbey record in 1725 that fifteen guineas were to be paid towards his release from prison, where he was confined for debt. He was buried in the south cloister of the Abbey. He is commonly credited with the invention of the double chant, the beautiful chant in G minor associated with his name being the earliest example known. This composition, however, was not original with him. He adapted it from a psalm-tune published in Allison's Psalter (1599), and subsequently in Playford's *Whole Booke of Psalms* (1677). Dr. Crotch printed the chant in his Collection of 1842, as 'from a harmony by Flintoft'. It first appeared in 1769, in *Fifty Double and Single Chaunts, being the most favourite as performed at St. Paul's, Westminster, and most of the cathedrals in England*, which is thought to be the first regular collection of chants made in this country.

90. CHANT (D) IN g.

FOSTER, JOHN (Staines, 1827–1915, Hampstead), was a pupil of Sir George Elvey at St. George's Chapel, Windsor; became organist of St. Andrew's, Wells Street, London, and established there the cathedral type of service; and in 1856 was appointed a lay vicar of Westminster Abbey. He was conductor of the Civil Services Musical Society and of other similar organizations. He had a fine tenor voice, and became a gentleman of the Chapel Royal. He published a *Gloria in Excelsis* to match and complete Orlando Gibbons's Service in F (1852); *Psalms and Hymns adapted to the Church of England* (1865); *Tunes for the Psalms and Hymns* (1864); *The Choral Harmonist* (1872).

39. CHANT IN E.   41. CHANT IN E.
40. CHANT IN f♯.

FOSTER, FREDERICK WILLIAM, was born at Bradford, not Bedford.

FRECH, JOHANN GEORG (Stuttgart, 1790–1864, Esslingen), was son of a watch-maker and organ-seller, and was educated at Stuttgart. At first he showed no inclination towards music, but later, a taste for singing and organ-playing developed and became a passion. In 1806 he became a teacher in the village school at Degerloch, near Stuttgart, and while there studied harmony, composition, violin, flute, and 'cello. In 1811 he became master in a model school erected at Esslingen for Protestant teachers; and in 1820 organist and director of the music of the principal church in Stuttgart. There he had to direct the music of the pupils of the seminary. In 1832 the Government appointed him inspector of the organs in the arrondissement of the Necker; and in the following year he was called to the direction of the music-school at Esslingen, where he remained till 1845. With Kocher and Silcher he edited a *Book of Chorales for Four Voices*. He also published a German Mass for Four Voices, cantatas, a grand opera *Montezuma*, and instrumental music.

26. ASPURG.

FUSSELL, PETER (?, 1750–1802, Winchester), was a pupil of James Kent at Winchester, and succeeded him there in 1774 in the double office of organist of the Cathedral and the College. He taught a number of musicians who subsequently made their mark, among them Charles Dibdin, sen. His Service in A was once popular, and he composed other church music which was appreciated in its day. He was buried in the north transept of the Cathedral.

128. CHANT IN G.

GARRATT, CHARLES A., according to an article by C. E. Miller, composer of WALDRONS, in *Musical Opinion*, Sept. 1933, on 'Some Organists I have known', was a pupil of Thomas Badsmore, organist at Lichfield (1833–81), and was himself teaching in London 1870–1, being then organist of St. Peter's, Croydon. He died at Toronto, in what year cannot now be discovered.

GAUNTLETT, HENRY JOHN, Mus.Doc. In his early childhood at Olney there was only a village band, in the west gallery of the church, to lead the singing. The vicar urged the parishioners to buy an organ and promised to supply an organist. His purpose was that his two girls, Arabella, aged 13, and Lydia, aged 10, should play the hymns, chants, and voluntaries, arranged as duets, as he was afraid that one child would not be able to produce sufficient effect in the large church. But Henry, aged 9, solemnly informed his father that 'it was not fitting for girls to take such a prominent part in the service of the sanctuary, and that if his mother would teach him to play, he would be ready to take the service by the time the organ was built'. Six months later he was as good as his word. Thomas Wright of Olney had this from Miss Gauntlett.

GAWTHORN, NATHANIEL, was clerk, that is, conductor of psalmody, at the Friday lecture in Eastcheap, early in the eighteenth century. In 1730 he published a collection of psalm-tunes in four parts, with some hymn-tunes and anthems, and an Introduction to Psalmody, under the title *Harmonia Perfecta, a complete collection of psalm tunes in four parts, fitted to all the various measures now in use, taken from all the most eminent masters.*

*91. NEWARK.

GIBBONS, CHRISTOPHER, Mus.Doc. (Westminster, 1615–76, Westminster), was the second son of Orlando, by whose genius he was overshadowed. He was not ten years old when his father died, and for a time he was in the care of his uncle Edward Gibbons, who was organist of Exeter Cathedral. There he came to know Matthew Locke, with whom he afterwards collaborated in the music for Shirley's masque *Cupid and Death* (1638), one of the most elaborate of such compositions. He became one of the children of the Chapel Royal. From 1638 till the Rebellion in 1644 he was organist of

Winchester Cathedral. 'When the dean and prebends fled', on the outbreak of the Civil War, 'he accompanied them and served in one of the garrisons' on the Royalist side. During the Commonwealth he earned his living by teaching the organ and playing the virginal. At the Restoration he was one of the few organists of the Chapel Royal at the time of Charles I's death who came forward to claim their posts. 'Modern illustrations of the Seven Sleepers,' says Hullah, 'they woke up in a world for whose ways they had no preparation—old-fashioned people, learned in Canon and believing in the ecclesiastical modes, called upon to furnish material for the Chapel and Chamber Royal.' Evelyn in his *Diary* indicates how complete the change was: 'Instead of ye antient, grave and solemn wind music accompanying ye organ, was introduc'd a concert of 24 violins between every pause, after ye French fantastical light way, better suiting a tavern, or a play-house, than a church.' Gibbons, however, was a great favourite of the King. According to Wood, he was 'a grand debauchee. He would often sleep at Morning Prayers when he was to play the organ.' In 1660 he was appointed organist to the Chapel Royal and private organist to the King; in the same year, organist of Westminster Abbey; and in 1663, at the express request of the King, received the Mus.Doc. degree from Oxford. He wrote a large number of string fantasias and some anthems.

23. CHANT IN G.

GOOCH, FREDERICK, D.C.L. (?, 1804–87, Baginton), son of the Rev. John Gooch, Archdeacon of Sudbury and rector of Benacre, became a Fellow of All Souls, Oxford, and for fifty-four years was rector of Baginton, a small village about two miles south of Coventry and three north-east of Kenilworth. His interest in music is evident from the fact that his name appears in the list of subscribers to S. S. Wesley's *European Psalmist* (1872). 'Old inhabitants of Baginton still speak of Dr. Gooch's fondness for and skill in matters musical.'

GOODENOUGH, ROBERT PHILIP (Ealing, 1776–1826, ?), second son of Samuel Goodenough, D.C.L. (Dean of Rochester, 1802, Bishop of Carlisle, 1808–27, a noted botanist in his day), was educated at Westminster School, of which his younger brother afterwards (1819–28) was headmaster, and at Christ Church, Oxford; B.A. 1796, M.A. 1799; married a daughter of Dr. William Markham, Archbishop of York, who preferred him in 1805 to the Prebend of Fenton in York Minster, and in 1806 to the rectory of Carlton-in-Lindrick, Notts. He is an example of the shameless pluralism that prevailed in the Church in those days, for on the same day on which he was inducted to his living in Nottinghamshire, he was installed in the Prebend of Hallaughton in the Collegiate Church (later Cathedral) of Southwell; in 1811 his father appointed him to the second Prebend in Carlisle Cathedral; in the same year he was given a similar stall in Ripon Minster; and in 1819 the Chapter of Southwell appointed him Rector of Beelsby, near Grimsby. After the evil fashion of the time he retained all these preferments till his death. It is probable that he never visited Beelsby except to be inducted to the living. He composed at least four double chants: in A and G (J. St. B. Joule's *Collection of Chants*); in F minor and in F (*The Cathedral Psalter*).

74–12. CHANT (D) IN F.

GOODSON, RICHARD, Mus.Bac. (?, 1655–1718?), was a well-known figure in the musical life of Oxford in his day. Trained as a chorister in St. Paul's Cathedral, he became organist of New College, Oxford, and Choragus, or superintendent of the music students' practice, in 1682, and in 1691 organist of Christ Church and Professor of Music in the University. In the professorship his son succeeded him in 1718. His chants are in a florid style. See Cowper's essay *The Village to the Town*.

15. CHANT IN C.

GRACE, HARVEY, Mus.Doc. (Cantuar.), has since 1931 been organist and director of the choir in Chichester Cathedral. He has published, in addition to the works named in the *Handbook*: *Ludwig van Beethoven*; *The Organ Works of Rheinberger*; *A Musician at Large*; *A Handbook for Choralists*.

GRANT, DAVID (Aberdeen, 1833–93, London), was a tobacconist in Union Street, Aberdeen. He had keen musical interest, and skill as well, for he scored parts for instrumental bands, and arranged tunes for *The Northern Psalter*. 'Here', he said one day to William Carnie, then editing that Psalter in parts, 'here, pit that in your bookie'—giving him the MS. of a new long-metre tune. 'What shall we call it?' 'Anything you like.' 'Well, seeing you deal so successfully in the weed, what do you say to naming it after the introducer of that article?' 'Good,' and so *Raleigh* the tune became. Grant was a well-read man and an interesting conversationalist, Carnie says in his *Reminiscences*. He was a member of the Footdee (pronounced Fittie in Aberdeen) church and choir. A song sung by his friends there contained this verse:

> Then if our frien' should ever dee
>   And seek the unkent valley, O,
> His epitaph it read shall be
>   From Bon Accord to Callao;
> Auld Fittie bell shall mournfu' ring
> While o'er his grave our heads we hing,
> And softly, slowly, sadly sing
>   Sweet Crimond and then Raleigh, O.

47. CRIMOND.

Biographical Notes

GRAY, ALAN (York, 1855–), was educated at St. Peter's School, York, and Trinity College, Cambridge. At first he intended to follow law, and took the degrees of LL.B. and LL.M.; but after studying under Dr. E. G. Monk, he devoted himself to music. He was musical director of Wellington College from 1883 until in 1892 he succeeded Stanford as organist of his old college and as conductor of the Cambridge Musical Society. He resigned in 1912. He has produced cantatas, *The Widow of Zarephath*, *Arethusa*, *The Legend of the Rock Buoy Bell*, *The Vision of Belshazzar*, *A Song of Redemption*; also *Odysseus in Phaeacia*; *An Easter Ode*; a Festival Te Deum; and compositions for the organ. He has acted as one of the editors of the Purcell Society. In 1926 he published *A Book of Descants*, from which the following are taken:

51. *DUNDEE.	85. *MARTYRDOM.	114. *ST. MAGNUS.
164. *FRANCONIA.	12. *MELCOMBE.	115. *ST. MARY.
61. *FRENCH.	13. *OLD HUNDREDTH.	144. *WILTSHIRE.
	82. *LONDON NEW.	105. *ST. FLAVIAN.

GRAY, HERBERT BRANSTON, D.D., was headmaster of Louth, not Routh, Grammar School. He died in 1929.

GREGORY NAZIANZEN retired to Nazianzus, then to Arizanz.

GRIFFITH, WILLIAM, d. Leicester, 1929.

GRIMSHAW, JOHN, was a Manchester musician. His *Twenty-four Hymns* was dedicated to the rector of St. John's, Manchester; so it is probable that he was organist at that church.

GURNEY, DOROTHY FRANCES, d. London, 1932.

HARINGTON, HENRY, M.D. (Kelston, Somersetshire, 1727–1816, Bath), son of Henry Harington of Kelston, who inherited that estate in 1726, was educated at Queen's College, Oxford, first with a view to holy orders, then for the medical profession; B.A., M.A., M.D. Settling as a physician at Wells in 1753, he moved in 1771 to Bath, where he became one of the best-known public figures; in 1793 he was alderman and mayor, serving in these offices with high credit. He had some poetic talent; he wrote a legend of the Cheddar Cliffs, entitled 'The Witch of Wokey', which subsequently found a place in Percy's *Reliques*. He had great charm of manner, which, according to a Bath historian, did his patients as much good as his medicines. J. T. Lightwood, in *The Music of the Methodist Hymn-Book*, says: 'For many years the good doctor was a conspicuous figure in the streets of Bath, recognized everywhere by his well-defined features and his eccentric old-fashioned garb. Tall, thin, and with an inclination to stoop as he walked, he looked older than his age warranted. He wore the triangular hat and the powdered full-bottomed wig of an earlier period; the whole of his

suit—his court dress, deep-pocketed waistcoat, and knee-breeches—
were all cut from the same sombre-hued cloth, and when he went
out walking he invariably held his handkerchief to his mouth as
a perpetual preventive against chills.' His leisure was largely devoted
to musical pursuits; he founded the Harmonic Society of Bath, and
was honoured with the title of its 'composer and physician'. He
published three books of glees, and a sacred dirge for Passion Week.
He was buried at Kelston, but there is a cenotaph to his memory in
Bath Abbey, with an organ and a passage from his dirge, 'Eloi,
Eloi, lama sabachthani', engraved upon it with this inscription:
'Dr. Harington / Medicus solers et fidelis / Poeta lepidus / Musicus
sciens et peritus / Magistratus gravis justus acer / Erga suos
amantissimus / Erga omnes comis et benevolus.'

66. HARINGTON.

HARRISON, RALPH, published the two volumes of his *Sacred
Harmony* in 1784 and 1791.

HART, JOSEPH, published the first edition of his *Hymns* in 1759.
Dr. Johnson, in his *Prayers and Meditations*, writes: 'On Easter
Day, 22nd April, 1764, I went to church (St. Clement Danes).
I gave a shilling: and seeing a poor girl at the Sacrament in a bed-
gown, gave her privately a crown, though I saw Hart's *Hymns* in
her hand.'

HARTSOUGH, LEWIS, died at Mount Vernon, Indiana, in 1919.
The year given in the *Handbook* for his death (1872) was the year
of the composition of his hymn and tune.

HATCH, EDWIN, was Professor of Classics in Trinity College,
Toronto (not Quebec).

HAYES, PHILIP, Mus.Doc. (Shrewsbury, 1738–97, London), was
probably educated by his father, Dr. William Hayes (q.v.). He
took his Mus.Bac. degree in 1763, became one of the gentlemen of
the Chapel Royal in 1769; organist of New College, Oxford, 1776;
of Magdalen, 1777; of St. John's, 1790. He was 'a monopolist of
organs', for he held these three posts simultaneously, and was,
besides, organist of St. Mary's Church, and from 1777, when he
succeeded his father, Professor of Music in the University. He
was extremely corpulent, and supposed to be the hugest man in
England; 'Phil Chaise' was his nickname. 'In good humour and
appearance he was a complete representation of Shakespeare's fat
knight, Sir John Falstaff.' A relative thus summed up his character:
'Very fond of works of *vertu*: a lazy dog, fond of good living, in fact,
a gourmand: fine temper, good-looking handsome man.' A lazy
man, however, he cannot have been, judging by the number of the
positions he filled, the large number of services and anthems he

wrote, and his many transcriptions in score of earlier works. He wrote *Prophecy*, an oratorio (still in MS.); an Ode for St. Cecilia's Day; *Telemachus*, a masque; eight anthems, &c. He edited also *Harmonia Wiccamica*. He died in London, where he had gone to attend the Chapel Royal, and was buried in St. Paul's.

81. CHANT IN A.	*117*. CHANT IN C.
81–11. CHANT IN a.	*119–81*. CHANT IN E♭.

HENLEY, PHOCION (Wootton Abbots, Wilts., 1728–98, London), when at Oxford spent much of his time in the cultivation of music in company with his friend William Jones, afterwards of Nayland, the composer of the tune ST. STEPHEN. In 1759 he became rector of St. Andrew-by-the-Wardrobe with St. Anne's, Blackfriars. In conjunction with Thomas Sharp he published *Divine Harmony: being a Collection of Psalm and Hymn Tunes in score*, 2 vols. (1798). He also composed chants and anthems, and a set of six hymns entitled *The Cure of Saul*.

29. CHANT (D) IN E♭.

HERMAN, NICOLAUS—also HEERMANN—(*c.* 1485–1561), was cantor of Joachimsthal, a place that grew up in a night when silver began to be mined there in 1556. The silver obtained was so famous that the German word *thaler* is taken from the last syllable of the name of the town. Herman was a poet and scholar as well as a musician; his verse has much the same kind of *naïveté* as that of Hans Sachs. He became cantor in 1518. In 1559 he spoke of himself as an old man, and in 1560 said he had not many more years to live; whence it has been inferred that he was then about 75 years of age. A number of chorales are extant of which he wrote both words and music. In the municipal library at Joachimsthal there is a folio containing all his songs.

108. ST. GEORGE.

HEYWOOD, JOHN (Birmingham, 1841– ?), studied at the R.A.M.; became organist of St. Jude's, Birmingham, in 1863; of St. Mary's, Aston Brook, and of the Plainsong Choir in Holy Trinity, Bordesley, in 1864; of St. Margaret's, Ward End, in 1865; and of St. Paul's, Balsall Heath, in 1856. He acted as organizing choirmaster of the Church Choral Association for the Archdeaconry of Coventry from 1871 to 1895, and in the latter year became chief inspector for the same Archdeaconry. For some time he was on the staff of *The Choir and Saturday Musical Review* and of *The Monthly Musical Record*. He composed chants, hymn-tunes, songs, anthems; and edited *The Anglican Psalter Noted* (1864) and *The Choral Office of Matins and Evensong* (1876).

101. CHANT IN E♭.

Biographical Notes

HILES, HENRY, Mus Doc. (Shrewsbury, 1826–1904, Worthing), was organist successively at Shrewsbury, Bury, Bishop Wearmouth; St. Michael's, Wood Street, and the Blind Asylum, Manchester; Bowden; St. Paul's, Manchester. In 1876 he became Lecturer in Harmony and Composition in Owens College, Manchester, and three years later in the Victoria University; and in 1893 a professor at Manchester College of Music. He was owner and editor of *The Quarterly Musical Review*. His works included oratorios, cantatas, anthems; a *Grammar of Music* (1879); and a book on *Harmony of Sounds* (1871).

24–7. CHANT IN A.   30. CHANT IN A♭.
76. CHANT IN B♭.

HINDLE, JOHN (Westminster, 1761–96, London), matriculated at Oxford in 1791 and took his Mus.Bac. degree. He became a lay vicar of Westminster Abbey. He was chiefly a song-writer, publishing a *Collection of Songs for 1 and 2 Voices* (1790), and a *Set of Glees for 3, 4, and 5 Voices*, in the same year.

86. CHANT IN G.

HOLDROYD, ISRAEL (*fl.* first half of eighteenth century), used the pseudonym *Philo-Musicae*. He published *The Spiritual Man's Companion, or the Pious Christian's Recreation, containing an historical Account of Music, &c.*; *Grounds of Music and Composition in all branches, . . . Psalm and Hymn Tunes* (2nd edition, 1733); *Chants and Anthems* (1733), and other works.

119. *ST. NICHOLAS.

HOLST, GUSTAV, died in 1934, and was buried in Chichester Cathedral, immediately under the memorial tablet to Weelkes, who, with Purcell, among English composers, stood highest in his admiration. The music at his funeral included his own 'Turn back, O Man' and 'This have I done'; Weelkes's 'Let Thy merciful ears'; and Vaughan Williams's Mass in G minor, and 'Let us now praise famous men'.

HOSMER, FREDERICK LUCIAN, D.D., d. Berkeley, California, in 1929.

HULL, ELEANOR HENRIETTA, D.Litt. (b. 1860), is daughter of Edward Hull, LL.D., the eminent geologist. She was long on the staff of *The Literary World*, contributed to Hastings's *Encyclopaedia of Religion and Ethics*; was one of the founders of the Irish Text Society, and for some time was secretary of the Royal Asiatic Society; is a member of the Council of the Folklore Society, and editor of the *Lives of the Celtic Saints* series, &c.

HUMPHREYS, PELHAM—Humphrey also, or Humfrey (he spelt his name all three ways)—(?, 1647–74, Windsor), was a chorister of the Chapel Royal under Captain Henry Cook, 1660–4, then was sent abroad by Charles II to pursue his studies, which he did chiefly in Paris under Lully. He was appointed in 1665 musician for the lute in the royal band; in 1666 a gentleman of the Chapel Royal; in 1672 master of the choristers. He was also 'composer in ordinary for the violins to His Majesty'. In 1667 Pepys records in his Diary: 'Home, and there find, as I expected . . . little Pelham Humphreys, lately returned from France, and is an absolute Monsieur, as full of form and confidence and vanity, and disparages everything and everybody's skill but his own. But to hear how he laughs at the King's music here . . . that they cannot keep time or tune nor understand anything . . . and that he and the King are mighty great.' He imported into church music the lighter style he learned from Lully, and introduced the instrumental symphonies which so delighted the King. He began early to compose, five of his anthems appearing in Clifford's *Divine Service and Anthems* in 1664, while he was still one of the Children of the Chapel Royal. At the same stage, along with Blow and Turner (q.v.), fellow choristers, he helped to compose what is known as the Club Anthem, which they intended to be a memorial of their friendship. Several fine anthems by him are in Boyce's *Cathedral Music*. Many of his songs remain. He is said to have written the words for many of the songs set by other composers of his time, and to have had 'as fanciful a wit as he had a delicate hand with the lute'. He sang 'tenner' also. He was a man of such great and various ability that his early death was a heavy loss to music. In a less pleasure-loving age doubtless his life would not have ended so soon. As it was, his work was of great importance, showing marked originality and charm. He introduced many new and beautiful effects into his compositions. Boyce says that he was the first of our ecclesiastical composers who had 'the least idea of musical pathos in expression of the words'. 'In his grave', says Sir W. H. Hadow, 'as in that of a greater musician than he, were buried "a rich possession and still fairer hopes".'

150. CHANT IN C.

HURST, WILLIAM, d. Coalville, 1934. His last composition was a tune to 'How sweet the name of Jesus sounds', written the day before his death. At his own request it was sung at his funeral.

IRELAND, JOHN, Mus.Doc. (Dunelm.).

JONES, EDITH (Lower Norwood, 1849–1929, Croydon).

JONES, JOHN (?, 1728–96, London), became organist of the Temple Church in 1749; of Charterhouse, in succession to Dr. Pepusch, in 1752; and of St. Paul's Cathedral in 1755. He held all three offices simultaneously. He was one of the directors of the Handel Commemoration in 1784. He was buried in the Charterhouse. He published several sets of harpsichord lessons, and in 1785 *Sixty Chants, Single and Double*. The *English Musical Gazette* of January 1819 said of him: 'Jones . . . appears not to have been worthy of his situation, for he was not capable of doing the duty for a length of time after the appointment; and as he could not play from score, he employed himself in arranging the Anthems in two lines. The same book is now in use at the Cathedral.' Of his well-known Double Chant in D, Haydn, who noted it down and in doing so improved it, said: 'A week before Whitsuntide I heard 4,000 children sing in St. Paul's Cathedral. . . . No music for a long time affected me so much as this innocent and reverential strain.' Not all his chants, however, were of this quality. The majority of them 'are florid and undevotional, "streams of crotchets", as Dr. Crotch would have said, also dotted quavers being freely used in the prevailing taste of the late Georgian period'.

73. CHANT (D) IN A.

JOSEPH, or JOSEPHI, GEORG. Add to the tunes noted as from *Heilige Seelenlust*:

38. CULBACH.

JOWETT, JOSEPH, published also *Musae Solitariae*, 2 vols. (1823), as 'a help to devotion, in the closet or the domestic circle', all the melodies being of his own composition. He also published *Verses on Various Occasions for Friends*, short poems, chiefly on musical subjects, printed for private circulation.

KEBLE, JOHN, is generally supposed to have been merely gentle, quiet, meek. As a fact, says Canon E. F. Smith of Tewkesbury, he was meek only in the sense in which Moses was meek. His 'meekness, which was almost a passion, veiled the inflexibility of a soldier sworn to hold the fort. In all emergencies his judgement turned instinctively to the course that was most daring and most dangerous. It was natural to him to take the line that would demand the severest strain. . . .

'It is Keble who most fully represents the peculiar *ethos* of the English Church.'—*Church Quarterly Review*.

It is curious to reflect, when the enormous popularity of *The Christian Year* is considered, that Parker, the well-known Church publisher, refused to give £60 for it when it was offered him, and indeed declined to publish it at all. The sale of it was prohibited in 1866 by the 'Dublin Commission for Discountenancing Vice', whose action, strangely, was approved by Archbishop Trench, himself a poet of no mean order.

KELWAY, THOMAS (Chichester, ?–1749, Chichester), was trained as a chorister in Chichester Cathedral, where he was probably a pupil of John Reading, whom he succeeded as lay vicar and organist, first 'on probation', in 1720, then properly 'sworn', in 1733. Seven services and nine anthems by him are contained in a MS. in Chichester Cathedral. Three of the services have been published— in B minor, A minor, and G minor; and of these J. S. Bumpus says, 'It may be confidently said that they are in use in every cathedral in England.' The burial-place of Kelway in the south aisle of the Cathedral was long lost to knowledge. When it was discovered and the stone replaced in 1846, Charles Crocker, the Bishop's verger— a remarkable man who published a volume of creditable poems— wrote the following sonnet:

Kelway! thy memory, fresh as vernal day
　　In many a heart's most secret holiest cell,
　　Where love of sacred song delights to dwell,
Lives, and shall live while music holds her sway
Within these hallowed walls where, day by day,
　　Year after year, he plied the wondrous art
　　Which bids the spirit from its prison start
And soar awhile to happier realms away.
His strains full oft still fall upon the ear
　　Of those who tread yon aisle, while at their feet
His name and record of his hope appear.
　　Peace to his ashes—be his slumbers sweet,
Till that glad morn when he shall wake to hear
The angel choir in nightless heaven's bright sphere.

76, 113. CHANT IN D. 　　　　28. CHANT IN G.
77. CHANT IN g.

KEN, THOMAS. To the hymns under his name add—257: 'All praise to Thee who safe hast kept'.

KNAPP, WILLIAM. His portrait hangs in the vestry of Wareham Church.

LAMPE, JOHANN FRIEDRICH, was bassoonist in Covent Garden Theatre, the wife of the proprietor of which was a convert of Charles Wesley. (See note on GOPSAL in this Supplement.) Charles thought highly of him and of his tunes; he published a volume of 24 of his own hymns set to Lampe's music. In *Sacred Melody* about 20 tunes are from Lampe's hand, chiefly set to 'peculiar metres'. They are for the most part florid and lively. With the exception of KENT they are rarely heard now. See note on IRISH, Hymn 153, in this Supplement; also *The Music of the Methodist Hymn-Book*, pp. 275-7.

LANGDON, RICHARD (Exeter, *c.* 1729–1803, Exeter), was grand-son of a priest-vicar of Exeter Cathedral. In 1753 he became organist and sub-chanter there, and was succeeded in 1777 by

William Jackson, composer of the setting of the Te Deum known as Jackson in F. In that year Langdon became organist of Ely Cathedral; in the following year of Bristol Cathedral; and in 1782 of the Cathedral of Armagh, where he remained till 1794, when he resigned and was succeeded by Dr. John Clarke, afterwards Clarke-Whitfeld. He published *Twelve Glees* (1770); two books of songs, &c.; and *Divine Harmony, a Collection, in Score, of Psalms and Anthems* (1774), in which the Double Chant in F, usually attributed to him, appeared anonymously.

37. CHANT (D) IN F.

LEE, WILLIAM (?, –1754,?), was organist of Southwell Cathedral from 1718 till his death.

93. CHANT IN G.

LEMON, JOHN (Truro, 1754–1814, Polvellen, near Looe), was an officer in the Horse Guards, attaining the rank of lieutenant-colonel. He became M.P. for West Looe in 1784, but applied for the Chiltern Hundreds in the same year. From 1786 to 1790 he was M.P. for Saltash, and subsequently for Truro, in four successive Parliaments, until his death. He was colonel of the Cornish Miners, and in 1804 a Lord Commissioner of the Admiralty.

19. CHANT (D) IN G.

LEY, HENRY GEORGE, M.A., Mus.Doc., was precentor of St. Peter's College, Radley, 1916–17; organist of Christ Church Cathedral, Oxford, 1919–26; Choragus of the University of Oxford, 1923–6; and is now precentor and musical instructor, Eton College, professor of the organ, Royal College of Music, and president of the Royal College of Organists. He was joint editor of *The Oxford Psalter* and *The Church Anthem Book*.

LITTLEDALE, RICHARD FREDERICK, LL.D., D.C.L. In *The English Reformers* (1933) this is said of him: 'Behind his Dublin eloquence and his inimitable Dublin wit, was a profound spirituality which brought to his confessional as many penitents as came to Pusey himself; behind them too were a powerful brain, an extraordinarily retentive memory, and great learning.'

LLOYD, JOHN MORGAN, Mus.Doc., Dublin.

LONGFELLOW, SAMUEL. It was in connexion with the beginning of his ministry at Fall River in 1848 that H. W. Longfellow wrote the beautiful 'Hymn for my Brother's Ordination', beginning:

> Christ to the young man said, 'Yet one thing more;
> If thou wouldst perfect be,
> Sell all thou hast and give it to the poor,
> And come and follow me.'

LUTTEROTH, Ascan Henri Théodore, contributed only seven tunes to the definitive edition of *Chants Chrétiens*.

MACALISTER, Robert Alexander Stewart. In the note on him *Temair Bug* should be *Temair Breg*. Prof. Macalister was organist of Adelaide Road Presbyterian Church, Dublin, 1920-7.

MACBEAN, Lachlan, d. 1931, Kirkcaldy.

McDONALD, Alexander (Edinburgh, *c.* 1770-?), was precentor of Old Greyfriars Church, Edinburgh, from 1803 till 1817. He succeeded one John Neil, who was dismissed by the Town Council from his office as 'uptaker o' the Psalm' because the Kirk Session made complaint that 'he had last Sunday fallen asleep in the desk during the time of the forenoon service, and was with great difficulty wakened, and could not sing the Psalm till the minister was obliged to give out the Psalm a second time'. McDonald also had to be dismissed after fourteen years' service for not attending to his duties. From 1807 to 1810 he was joint music master with Archibald McDonald, presumably his father, at George Heriot's Hospital, Edinburgh. He edited and published in 1807 *A Collection of Vocal Music, containing Church Tunes, Anthems, and Songs, for the Use of the several Hospitals of the City*; and is believed to have edited also *The Notation of Music Simplified* (Glasgow, 1826).

68. HERIOT'S TUNE.

MACNICOL, Nicol, D.Litt., D.D., has now retired from missionary work in India. He was Wilde Lecturer in Natural and Comparative Religion in the University of Oxford, 1932-4, and holds a lectureship in Hartford Seminary, U.S.A., 1934-5. To his other books add: *What Jesus means for Men*; *India in the Dark Wood*; *The Living Religions of the Indian People*.

MANN, Arthur Henry, d. 1929, Cambridge.

MASTERMAN, John Henry Bertram, d. 1933, Stoke Damerel.

MATHAMS, Walter John, d. 1931, Swanage.

MATHER, William (?, 1756-1808, Sheffield), was organist of St. Paul's and St. James's, Sheffield.

In 1806 he issued from his own house in 11 Norfolk Row *Sacred Music*, containing 26 tunes and 6 anthems. Some of his tunes had previously appeared in other publications, but as they were not always correctly printed he published this book in order that mistakes might be rectified.

His son John (Sheffield, 1781-1850, Edinburgh), after serving for a time as organist of Sheffield Parish Church, removed to Edinburgh, about 1810, and thereafter was one of the most prominent musicians in that city. He composed *Hail to the Chief*, a glee, songs, &c.

126. SHEFFIELD.

MATTHEWS, SAMUEL, Mus.Bac. (?, 1796–1832, Cambridge), was trained as a chorister in Westminster Abbey under Robert Cooke. Afterwards he was a lay clerk of Winchester Cathedral. In 1822 he was appointed organist of Trinity and St. John's Colleges, Cambridge, in succession to William Beale, the distinguished madrigal writer. William Glover, in his *Memoirs of a Cambridge Chorister*, says that he was 'a kindly man in private, but a regular martinet during official hours'. He composed a Service in D, and published four anthems from the works of Haydn, Mozart, and others.

84. CHANT (D) IN E.

MILTON, JOHN (Milton, near Halton and Thame, Oxfordshire, *c.* 1563–1646/7, London), son of a well-to-do yeoman of Stanton St. John, near Oxford, was 'cast out by his father, a bigoted Roman Catholic, for abjuring the Roman tenets'. He is believed to have been, before this, at Christ Church, Oxford. Going to London to seek his fortune, he was apprenticed to a member of the Scriveners' Company in 1595, and in 1599 or 1600 was admitted to the freedom of the Company. Thirty-four years later he was elected Master of the Company, but did not accept office. In his house in Bread Street in the City his poet son grew up in an atmosphere of music. Masson in his *Life* of the poet suggests that the father practised music professionally, but that is unlikely, in view of the eminence to which he rose in his profession and the considerable fortune he made in it. He was able to retire about 1632 to Horton, Bucks.; later, he lived at Reading, and in 1643 returned to London to live with his son in the Barbican. There he died, and was buried in St. Giles', Cripplegate. A madrigal by him—*Fair Oriana in the Morn*—appeared in *The Triumphes of Oriana*, and several of his songs for three voices are in Leighton's *Teares and Lamentacions*. He is said to have composed an *In Nomine* of forty parts, for which, according to his grandson Edward Phillips, on the authority of the poet, he was rewarded with a gold medal and chain by a Polish Prince to whom he presented it. For Ravenscroft's *Whole Booke of Psalmes* (1625) he harmonized two tunes, *Norwich* and *York*, the latter in two versions. His anthems have been reprinted by G. E. P. Arkwright. Milton pays tribute to his father's musical gifts in his poem *Ad Patrem*.

146.* YORK.

MONK, MARK JAMES, Mus.Doc., d. 1929, Blackheath.

MOORE, THOMAS. The last sentence of this note should read: He wrote the *Life of Byron*.

MORLEY, HENRY KILLICK. This note is inaccurate. The writer of the tune NEWCASTLE was Henry L. Morley, about whom little is known beyond the fact that he wrote another tune, named CHARLTON, for the same book, *The London Tune Book*, in which NEWCASTLE appeared. See note on Hymn 36.

MORLEY, WILLIAM, Mus.Bac. (d. 1731), was admitted a gentleman of the Chapel Royal, 1715. He composed some songs, but is now known only by his double chant in D minor, printed in Boyce's Collection. It is by some supposed to be the oldest double chant in existence.

77. CHANT (D) IN D MINOR.

MORNINGTON, EARL OF, Mus.Doc. (Dangan, Ireland, 1735–81, Kensington)—Garrett Colley Wellesley (Wesley)—was a born musician: with very little help he learned to play the organ and the violin and to compose. When he consulted Th. Rosengrave and Geminiani about further study, they informed him that he already knew all they could teach him. After graduating M.A. in Dublin, 1757, he founded in that year the Academy of Music, an amateur society in which ladies for the first time sang in the chorus. In 1764 he took his Mus.Doc. degree, and became Professor of Music in Dublin University. In 1758 he succeeded his father as Baron Mornington, and in 1760 was created Viscount Wellesley and Earl of Mornington. He was the father of the Duke of Wellington and the Marquis Wellesley. He excelled as a composer of glees. A complete collection of his glees and madrigals was edited by Sir Henry Bishop in 1846.

18. CHANT (D) IN D.

MOUNTAIN, JAMES, D.D., d. 1933, Tunbridge Wells.

NAYLOR, EDWARD WOODALL, Mus.Doc., d. 1934, Cambridge. He became Lecturer in Musical History in the University of Cambridge, in 1926. Besides the books mentioned, he wrote *The Poets and Music* (1928).

NEALE, JOHN MASON. These facts about this remarkable man may be added. At Sackville College, in spite of his troubles and derisory salary, he was 'supremely happy, with his pensioners, his five children, his books, his dreams, and the great Sussex Downs'. He is said to have been able to read, write, and think in twenty-one different languages. The Ancient section of *Hymns Ancient and Modern* was entirely his work. For some time he earned enough to pay for his children's governess by acting as a leader-writer for *The Morning Chronicle*.

NISBET, JOHN MACDONNELL, d. 1935, Aberdeen.

NOVELLO, VINCENT. Cf. Lamb's *Essays of Elia—A Chapter on Ears*, where Lamb speaks of 'my good Catholic friend Nov——;

who, by the aid of a capital organ, himself the most finished of players, converts his drawing-room into a chapel, his week-days into Sundays, and these into minor heavens'. This was Novello, who was a friend of all the Lamb group. His biography was written by his daughter.

OAKELEY, FREDERICK, D.D. Dean Church, in *The Oxford Movement*, says: 'Mr. Oakeley was perhaps the first to realize the capacities of the Anglican ritual for impressive devotional use, and his services, in spite of the disadvantages of the time and also of his chapel, are still remembered by some as having realized for them, in a way never since surpassed, the secrets and the consolations of the worship of the Church. Mr. Oakeley without much learning was master of a facile and elegant pen. He was a man who followed a trusted leader with chivalrous boldness, and was not afraid of strengthening his statements.'

OAKELEY, Sir HERBERT STANLEY, Mus.Doc. His father was Dean of Barking, not Bocking.

78. CHANT (Q) IN F.

PATRICK, ST. The birthplace is uncertain. On the whole, Abergavenny has most of the probabilities in its favour.

PURCELL, DANIEL (*c.* 1660–1717), younger brother of Henry, became organist of Magdalen College, Oxford, 1688–95, then settled in London. After Henry's death he was in great demand for the kind of work in which Henry excelled, the composition of music for plays; of this, a great deal survives. He was organist of St. Andrew's, Holborn, 1713–17. He published *The Psalmes set full for the Organ or Harpsichord as they are Plaid in Churches and Chappels in the manner given out; as also with their Interludes of great Variety.* One of the 'givings-out' and one of the interludes may be seen in *The Musical Times* for 1905.

4. CHANT IN G.

PURCELL, HENRY (?, 1658–95, London), son of a gentleman of the Chapel Royal and Master of the Choristers of Westminster Abbey, was trained as a choir-boy in the Chapel Royal, and studied under Cooke, Blow, and Humfrey, from whom he learned the new French style which Humfrey acquired from Lully. In 1679 he became organist of the Abbey, Blow resigning, it is said, in his favour. He is by many regarded as the greatest of English musicians. He touched the music of his age at every point, and in every department left great works; the large amount of music written by him in his short life is equalled by its variety. He wrote odes, incidental music for plays, *Dido and Aeneas*, 'the only perfect English opera ever written, and the only opera of the seventeenth century that is performed nowadays for the sheer pleasure it gives as opera', and a great mass of anthems and services, the greatest religious music of his time; also songs, duets, catches, music for organ, strings, harpsichord, &c. Even now a vast quantity remains in manuscript. At the end of his short life he was master of every branch of musical technique. His gift of melody has been excelled, some think, only by Mozart. It was from his work that Handel imbibed that English quality which distinguishes it. None of his church music was published in his lifetime, and until Vincent Novello began editing it in 1828, not more than a dozen of his anthems were known to exist in print.

> 7, *130*. CHANT IN a.
> *80*. CHANT (D) IN c.
> *38*, 55. CHANT (D) IN f.

PURCELL, Thomas (d. 1682), uncle of the great Henry Purcell, was appointed a gentleman of the Chapel Royal, 1660; copyist and lay vicar of Westminster Abbey, 1661; Composer in Ordinary for the Violins to the King, along with Pelham Humfrey; and Musician in Ordinary for the Lute and Voice, in succession to Henry Lawes, 1662; Master of the King's Band of Music, in conjunction with Humfrey, 1672. He composed several chants.

> *102*. CHANT IN g.
> *102–12*. CHANT IN G.
> *131*. CHANT IN G.

PYE, Kellow John, Mus.Bac. (Exeter, 1812–1901, Exmouth), entered the R.A.M. immediately upon its foundation, and took the first pianoforte lesson ever given within its walls, from Cipriani Potter; he studied there also under Crotch, and remained for six years. In 1830 he returned to Exeter and acquired a great reputation in the south-west of England as a music teacher. In 1832 he was awarded the Gresham medal for his full anthem 'Turn Thee again, O Lord'. In 1842 he took the Oxford Mus.Bac. degree. In 1853 he abandoned music as a profession and entered as a partner a wine merchant's business in London. In his new position, however, he was able to render great service to musical education and culture in the capital. He joined the directorate of the R.A.M., and was chairman of the committee of management; the executive of the National Training School of Music; the Committee of the Bach Choir; the Council of the R.C.M.; the Madrigal Society; the Mendelssohn Scholarship Foundation, &c. He published *Four Full Anthems, Three Short Full Anthems*, &c.

> *104*. CHANT (D) IN E.

RAYMOND-BARKER, Elizabeth (Leicester, 1829–1916, Hayward's Heath), daughter of William Hacket of Ayleston Hall, Leicester, married in 1853 the Rev. Frederic Mills Raymond-Barker,

M.A., of Oriel College, Oxford. She entered the Roman Church in 1867, when she took the additional names of Mary Agnes. At the request of J. M. Neale she composed tunes to his *Hymns of the Eastern Church* (1864–68); the first series (1864) contains six hymns, which she set to music at Bisley, Gloucestershire, in 1863. Her tune *Damascus*, set to Neale's hymn 'Those eternal bowers', was familiar in the 1899 edition of *The Church Hymnary*. Neale seems to have admired her work greatly. Of her setting to 'Safe home, safe home in port' he says: 'One feels that the anonymous writer of such a plaintive yet soothing melody, must have been one—to quote Abp. Trench's words with regard to the author of *Veni, Sancte Spiritus*— acquainted with great sorrow, but also with great consolation.'

44. CORONA.

RIDSDALE, CHARLES JOSEPH, d. 1929.

ROBERTS, LEWIS JONES, d. Aberayron, 1931.

RUSSELL, WILLIAM (London, 1777–1813, London), was deputy for his father as organist of St. Mary Aldermanbury, 1789–93; organist, Great Queen Street, Lincoln's Inn Fields, 1793–8, the chapel being sold to the Methodists in the latter year; organist of St. Ann's, Limehouse, 1798, and of the Foundling Hospital Chapel, 1801; pianist and composer at Sadler's Wells from 1800 for about four years. He had a high reputation as organist and pianist. He composed three oratorios, a Mass in C minor, glees, songs, spectacles, and pantomimes. In 1809 he published *Psalms, Hymns and Anthems for the Foundling Chapel.*

    136. CHANT IN C.   *107.* CHANT (D) IN E.
    122. CHANT IN G.   *9, 10.* CHANT (D) IN G.

RYLEY, GEOFFREY CHARLES EDWARD, vacated the living of Hadlow, Tonbridge, 1929, to become Domestic Chaplain to the Bishop of Rochester.

SAVAGE, WILLIAM (?, 1720–89, London), was a pupil of Dr. Pepusch. He became organist of Finchley Parish Church, and in 1744 one of the gentlemen of the Chapel Royal. In 1748 he became almoner, vicar-choral, and Master of the Boys (choristers) in St. Paul's Cathedral. In that office, it is on record, 'he does not appear to have preserved the amiable qualities of his predecessor (Charles King). As was his name, so was his nature, for we find that in 1773 it was deemed expedient to remove him, on account, it is said, of the great harshness with which he treated the boys committed to his charge.' He was a fine bass vocalist, and a capable organist. He published chants and other church music, but his reputation survives only by his single Chant in C.

129. CHANT IN C.

SCOTT-GATTY, Sir ALFRED. Among his hundreds of popular songs the best known in Scotland is 'Rothesay Bay', the words by Mrs. Craik.

SEVEN SOBS OF A SORROWFUL SOUL.—For William Hunnis's chequered career see *The Dictionary of National Biography*.

SHAW, GEOFFREY, Mus.Doc. (Cantuar.).

SHAW, MARTIN, Mus.Doc. (Cantuar.), edited, in addition to the works mentioned, *The English Carol Book*, and, jointly with R. Vaughan Williams, *The Oxford Book of Carols* (1928); in 1929 he published his autobiography under the title *Up till Now*.

SILAS, ÉDOUARD. J. A. Fuller-Maitland relates in *A Door-keeper of Music*, that when, as musical critic of *The Times* he was searching for some one to deputize for him, 'Many were the oddities among those who tried their hands at helping me; one, highly recommended, expressed the opinion that there was only one really great composer then living, in the person of a certain Édouard Silas, whose name may be read in the annals of the Philharmonic Society.'

SMART, Sir GEORGE THOMAS, Mus.Doc. (London 1776–1867, London), was educated under Ayrton, Dupuis, and Arnold; organist, St. James's Chapel, Hampstead Road; taught singing and harpsichord; knighted in 1811 by the Lord Lieutenant of Ireland for successful conducting of concerts in Dublin; was conductor of the Philharmonic Society's concerts for many years; one of the organists of the Chapel Royal, 1822; succeeded Attwood as composer to the Chapel Royal, 1838. He united great administrative ability with a genius for conducting, and for a long period of years was in great demand all over the country for conducting festivals; he introduced Mendelssohn's *St. Paul* to this country at Liverpool. He gave lessons in singing till he was over eighty, instructing among others Sontag and Jenny Lind in the traditional manner of singing Handel's songs. He edited Orlando Gibbons's madrigals for the Musical Antiquarian Society, and the *Dettingen Te Deum* for the Handel Society; and composed anthems, chants, psalm-tunes, &c. See *Leaves from the Journal of Sir George Smart*, published in 1907.

144. WILTSHIRE.

SMITH, JOHN STAFFORD (Gloucester, 1750–1836, London), son of an organist of Gloucester Cathedral, was taught by his father, then by Boyce, then as a chorister of the Chapel Royal under Nares. He was a distinguished organist, tenor singer, composer, and musical antiquary. In 1784 he became a gentleman of the Chapel Royal; 1785, lay vicar of Westminster Abbey; 1790, organist of Gloucester Musical Festival; 1802, one of the organists of the Chapel Royal in succession to Arnold; 1805, master of the choristers there.

His training of the boys was of a happy-go-lucky description. John Goss, who was one of them, having saved enough of his pocket-money to buy a copy of Handel's Organ Concertos, encountered Smith while carrying it under his arm. 'What is that you are carrying?' 'Only Handel's Organ Concertos, sir; I thought I'd like to learn to play them.' 'Oh, and pray, sir, did you come here to learn to play, or sing?' 'To sing, sir.' Whereupon the master seized the book, and hit the boy over the head with it. Goss never saw it again. Smith used to take Goss with him occasionally on his walks, and would unbend to him, telling him stories of his experiences and the people he had met. On returning home, 'he impressed his teaching on the skin of his pupil by a mild castigation. By this means his dignity as a master was maintained, he consoled himself for having unbent his mind to a junior, and felt that he had justified his position as a senior, according to the rule then prevalent with parents and guardians.' Smith was in the front rank of glee composers; he published five collections of glees alone. His chief publications were: *A Collection of English Songs, in score, for three and four voices, composed about the year 1500. Taken from MSS. of the same age* (this contains the Agincourt Song); *Musica Antiqua*, a collection of old music from the twelfth to the eighteenth century; he also assisted Sir John Hawkins, as Hawkins acknowledged in his Preface, in preparing his *History of Music*, by reducing ancient compositions to modern notation, and by lending MSS. from his remarkable library. After his death, this library was auctioned by a man who knew nothing of its value and had done nothing to let connoisseurs know of what it consisted, and most of its treasures were lost. In 1793 Smith published *Twelve Chants composed for the Use of the Choir Service of the Church of England*, and also a volume of anthems.

89–1. CHANT (D) IN G.
89–38. CHANT (D) IN g.

SMITH, SAMUEL FRANCIS, D.D., was an ardent advocate of foreign missions, would himself have become a foreign missionary if circumstances had not prevented him, and wrote eighteen missionary hymns. He wrote also two books on missions, *Missionary Sketches* and *Rambles in Missionary Fields*, the latter recording impressions of a visit to the missions of India, Ceylon, and Burma.

STANLEY, R. H. Of this composer nothing has been discovered.

40. CHANT IN A.

STEVENSON, Sir JOHN ANDREW, Mus.Doc. (Dublin, 1761–1833, Headfort House), was son of a violinist in the State Band, Dublin; chorister, Christ Church Cathedral, Dublin, 1771; in choir of St. Patrick's, 1775–80; vicar choral of St. Patrick's, 1783, and of

Christ Church, 1800. In 1791 he received the Mus.Doc. degree from Dublin University; in 1803 was knighted by the Lord Lieutenant, Lord Hardwicke; and in 1814 was appointed first organist and musical director of Dublin Castle Chapel. He died while on a visit to the Marchioness of Headfort. He composed a good deal for the stage; wrote an oratorio *Thanksgiving*, which was performed at the Dublin Musical Festival of 1831; published many glees, songs, canzonets, also (1825) a collection of services and anthems; but is best known by his symphonies and accompaniments to Moore's *Irish Melodies*. See note in this Supplement on HOWARD.

STEWART, CHARLES HYLTON, d. 1932, Windsor, two months after taking up duty as organist of St. George's Chapel there. He was organist of Chester Cathedral 1930–2.

STRONG, THOMAS BANKS, D.D., &c., Bishop of Oxford, is now G.B.E., Chancellor of the Order of the Garter and Clerk of the Closet; Visitor of Cuddesdon, Bradley, Radley, and Dorchester, and Warden of Ripon Hall, Oxford.

SWIFT, JAMES FREDERICK, d. 1931.

TATE, NAHUM. Southey, quoting from Oldys, says of Tate: 'He was a good-natured fuddling companion, and his latter days were spent in the Mint as a refuge from his creditors.'

THOMSON, ANDREW MITCHELL, D.D. (Sanquhar, 1778–1831, Edinburgh), was educated at the University of Edinburgh, was for a brief time schoolmaster at Markinch, Fife, and in 1802 was licensed by the Presbytery of Kelso and ordained at Sprouston. He was translated to the East Church, Perth, in 1808, and to New Greyfriars, Edinburgh, in 1810. In the following year he graduated as M.A. in the University there. Because of his outstanding pulpit gifts he was presented by the Town Council in 1814 to the newly erected church and parish of St. George's in the New Town of the city. Lord Cockburn, in his *Memorials of his Time*, referring to the poverty of town councils then, says: 'It was necessary to fill churches, for the sake of the seat rents; and churches could only be filled by putting in ministers for whom congregations would pay. This business principle operated seriously in Edinburgh, where the magistrates had laid out large sums in building and repairing kirks. This brought Andrew Thomson into this city; which was the opening of his career. His Whig reputation was so odious, that it rather seemed at one time as if civic beggary would be preferred to it; and most vehemently was his entrance into our untroubled fold opposed. But, after as much plotting as if it had been for the Popedom, he got in, and in a few years rewarded his electors by drawing about £1,800 a year for them; a fact which, of itself, loosened all the city churches

from the dead sea in which they were standing.' In ideas and enter-
prise he was far ahead of his time. An enthusiastic musical amateur,
he set himself to improve the psalmody of his church, and in 1823
did a great service to congregational singing generally by inducing
R. A. Smith (q.v.) to come from Paisley to be his precentor. He
encouraged Smith in every way. They had already collaborated
in the compilation of *Sacred Harmony, Part I, for the Use of
St. George's Church, Edinburgh* (1820), to which Thomson himself
contributed *Redemption* and *St. George's, Edinburgh*, and eleven
other tunes now forgotten. They again collaborated in *Sacred
Music, consisting of Tunes, Sanctuses, Doxologies, Thanksgivings, &c.,
Sung in St. George's Church, Edinburgh* (1825). Thomson was a
leading public figure in Edinburgh. He wrote copiously besides,
publishing many books of sermons and lectures. For twenty years
he edited *The Edinburgh Christian Instructor* (30 vols.), and he wrote
forty-three articles in *The Edinburgh Encyclopaedia*, of which he
was part proprietor. He died suddenly within a few steps of his
own door, when returning from a Presbytery meeting. His son
John became Professor of Music in the University of Edinburgh.

190. ST. GEORGE'S, EDINBURGH.

TOMLINSON, ——. Of this composer nothing has been discovered.
16. CHANT IN G.

TOPLADY, AUGUSTUS MONTAGUE. That there was little to choose
between the Wesleys and Toplady as disputants is shown by the fact
that John Wesley, irritated by the torrent of scurrilous pamphlets
from his opponent's pen, wrote: 'Mr. Augustus Toplady I know well;
but I do not fight with chimney-sweepers'; and Toplady wrote:
'Mr. Wesley and his subalterns are in general so excessively
scurrilous and abusive, that contending with them resembles fighting
with chimney-sweepers, or bathing in a mud pool.' Yet this same
virulent controversialist, when he lay dying at the age of thirty-eight,
answered a friend who suggested that he might recover, by saying,
'No, no. I shall die. For no mortal could endure such manifesta-
tions of God's glory as I have done, and live.'

TRAVERS, JOHN (?, 1703–58, London), was trained as a chorister
of St. George's, Windsor, under John Goldwin, and on leaving was
enabled by the generosity of Henry Godolphin, Dean of St. Paul's
and Provost of Eton College, to become an articled pupil of
Dr. Maurice Greene. He was assisted in his studies also by Dr.
Pepusch (chapelmaster to the 'magnificent' Duke of Chandos, and
afterwards (1737–52) organist of the Charterhouse; possessor of a
remarkable library, a learned theorist, and one of the first to study
English medieval music). About 1725 he became organist of St.
Paul's, Covent Garden, and concurrently of Fulham Church; in

1732, of the Chapel Royal. He copied, Burney says, Pepusch's 'correct, dry, and fanciless style'. Pepusch left him half of his fine musical library. Travers published *Eighteen Canzonets for two, and three, Voices*, the words chiefly from the posthumous works of Matthew Prior; *XII Voluntaries for the organ or harpsichord;* and *The Whole Book of Psalms for one, two, three, four, and five Voices, with a Thorough Bass for the Harpsichord*. 'Few pieces of liturgical music are so frequently drawn upon in our Cathedrals as "Travers in F".'

125. CHANT IN E.

TRENT, ——. Of this composer no particulars have been found.

25. CHANT (D) IN A♭.

TUCKER, WILLIAM—also TUCKERE and TUCKERS—(?, 1678, Westminster), was in holy orders, a gentleman of the Chapel Royal, and (1660) a minor canon and precentor of Westminster Abbey. His name appears many times in the accounts of payments to the royal musicians. It is surmised that he may have been a son of Edmund Tucker (*fl.* late sixteenth and early seventeenth century), who was organist of Salisbury Cathedral. Some of Edmund's works are believed to be among those attributed to William, which consisted of anthems, church services—a *Whole Service in F*, and an *Evening Service in F*.

124. CHANT IN A.

TURNER, WILLIAM, Mus.Doc. (Oxford, 1651–1739/40, Westminster), son of the cook at Pembroke College, Oxford, was trained as a chorister of Christ Church there, and afterwards at the Chapel Royal, where he had as fellow pupils John Blow and Pelham Humphreys (q.v.). The three friends collaborated during their time there in the composition of the Club Anthem. 'They agreed', Boyce says, 'each to set different verses, and to connect and form them into a regular performance; to remain as a memorial of their fraternal esteem and friendship.' Turner's contribution was a bass solo in the middle. He had a fine counter-tenor voice, and sang for a time in Lincoln Cathedral. Becoming a gentleman of the Chapel Royal in 1669, he served as such under seven kings and queens successively, 'and in the former part of his life his voice . . . recommended him to much favour'. He was also a vicar-choral of St. Paul's, and a lay vicar of Westminster Abbey. He received his Mus. Doc. degree from Cambridge in 1696. He composed songs and catches, many of which were popular in their day, operas, and a large quantity of church music, services and anthems. He also edited *Ravenscroft's Psalm Tunes* (1728). He died within four days of his wife, and they are buried together in the cloisters of the Abbey. On his tombstone there is engraved on an open book the canon set to the words of the Psalm in his Gamut Service. The inscription concludes: 'His own musical compositions, especially his church musick, are a far nobler monument to his memory than any other that can be raised for him.'

VINCENT, CHARLES JOHN, Mus.Doc., d. 1934.

WAINWRIGHT, ROBERT, Mus.Doc. (Stockport, 1748–82, Liverpool), was the eldest son of John Wainwright (q.v.). He gained the Mus.Doc. degree at Oxford, 1774, a *Te Deum* of his composition being performed at the graduation. He succeeded his father as organist of the Collegiate Church, Manchester, 1768, and in 1775 was appointed organist of St. Peter's (afterwards the cathedral), Liverpool. He composed an oratorio, *The Fall of Egypt*, anthems, services, &c. The rapidity of his execution on the organ was remarkable. Edward Miller, in his *History of Doncaster*, relates that on the erection of a new organ in Doncaster Church by Snetzler, Wainwright was a candidate for the post of organist. Among his six competitors was no less a person than F. W. Herschel, afterwards famous as Sir William Herschel, the astronomer, but then making his way as a musician in this country, having lately come from Germany. Wainwright had to play second before the judges, and Herschel third. 'Wainwright's execution was so rapid that old Snetzler ran about exclaiming, "Te tevil, te tevil, he run over te key like one cat; he will not give my piphes room for to shpeak!" During this performance Miller said to Herschel, "What chance have you to follow this man?" He replied, "I don't know, but I am sure fingers will not do." In due time he ascended the gallery, and drew from the organ such a full volume of slow solemn harmony as Miller could by no means account for. After a short extempore effusion of this character, he finished with the Old Hundredth tune, which he played better than his opponent had done. "Ay, ay!" cried Snetzler, "tish is very goot, very goot inteet; I vill luff tish man, for he gives my piphes room for to shpeak." Herschel being afterwards asked by Miller by what means he had produced so uncommon an effect, answered, "I told you fingers would not do"; and taking two pieces of lead from his waistcoat pocket, he said, "One of these I placed on the lowest key of the organ, the other on the octave above; thus, by accommodating the harmony, I gained the power of four hands instead of two." Herschel was thereupon appointed, but soon afterwards entered upon other pursuits, and the musician has been long forgotten in the astronomer.'

WALMISLEY, THOMAS ATTWOOD (London, 1814–56, Hastings), son of Thomas Forbes Walmisley, organist of the Female Orphan Asylum and of St. Martin's-in-the-Fields, studied under his god-father Attwood; became a brilliant pianist; organist of Croydon Church, 1830; of Trinity and St. John's Colleges, Cambridge, 1833; Mus.Bac. the same year; entered Corpus Christi College, where he distinguished himself in mathematics; while still in residence for the B.A. degree became Professor of Music in succession to Clarke-Whitfeld, 1836; B.A. two years later; M.A. 1841; Mus.Doc. 1848. In general culture as well as musical scholarship he was far ahead of most musicians of his time; he was also one of the first organists of his day. He was much overworked, as his Sunday engagements in Cambridge show: 7.15, St. John's College; 8, Trinity; 9.30, King's; 10.30, St. Mary's Church; 2, University Service, St. Mary's; 3.15, King's; 5, St. John's; 6.15, Trinity. He was highly strung and sensitive. Once he asked Mendelssohn, with whom he was on terms of friendship, to consider a symphony he had written. Mendelssohn, on learning that it was a first attempt, declined, saying, 'Let us see first what number 12 will be like'. Walmisley was so discouraged that he gave up orchestral writing altogether. He published *Cathedral Music*, a collection of anthems and services; a collection of chants; choral hymns in four parts; and a volume of his anthems and services was edited by his father after his death. 'The desire to be free from the burning current of his thoughts, which led he knew not whither,' led to his indulging unduly in sedatives to soothe his too active brain, and an overdose of one of these lethal remedies caused his death. He was buried in the beautiful churchyard of Fairlight. On the tablet to his memory in the ante-chapel of Trinity College, this phrase from the quartet of his noble anthem 'If the Lord Himself' is engraved: 'The snare is broken, and we are delivered.'

35. CHANT (D) IN F.
87. CHANT IN G.

WALTON, HERBERT FRANCIS RAINE, d. 1929, Glasgow.

WARING, ANNA LAETITIA, b. 1823.

WATT, LAUCHLAN MACLEAN, D.D., LL.D., was Moderator of the General Assembly of the Church of Scotland, 1933, and resigned the charge of Glasgow Cathedral, 1934.

WELDON, JOHN (Chichester, 1676–1736, London), received his education first as a chorister of Eton College, then as a pupil of Henry Purcell. His appointments were: 1694–1701, organist of New College, Oxford; 1701, gentleman extraordinary of the Chapel Royal; 1708, organist of the Chapel Royal in succession to Blow; 1715, second composer there. He was very popular as an organist, and held office in St. Bride's, Fleet Street, and St. Martin-in-the-Fields, concurrently with his other appointment. He received his appointment to the latter church out of compliment to George I, who had been elected churchwarden of this parish, in which he lived, but who tired of his duty in two months and presented the church with, as solatium for his withdrawal, an organ costing £1,500. Weldon wrote three books of songs, music for four operas, many anthems, and in particular published *Divine Harmony: Six Select Anthems for a Voice alone, with a Thorow Bass for the Organ, Harpsichord, or Arch-Lute*. In this book there is a picture of the interior of St. James's Chapel with service going on, in which the violists, lutenists, and 'Hoboy players' are shown playing left-handed. 'John Weldon wrote some exceedingly beautiful music for the Church, in which deep religious sentiment seems to have been his motive power. If it does not indicate a very masterly or comprehensive genius, it is distinguished by smooth harmony and a vocal elegance in its phrases which remains unimpaired even at the present day' (J. S. Bumpus, *History of English Cathedral Music*).

79. CHANT IN g.

WEST, LEWIS RENATUS (London, 1753–1826, Tytherton, Wiltshire), belonged to the United Brethren (Moravians), and for a time was a master in their school at Fulneck, Leeds. After a brief time as tutor and assistant preacher at Bedford, he settled in Dublin in 1784 as assistant minister, with special charge of the young men of the Moravian congregation. He was ordained as deacon in 1785, and after leaving Dublin was minister in succession of congregations in Gracehill, Ireland, Mirfield, Bath, Bristol, and Tytherton, where he died. He was buried in the Moravian burial-ground there. He was a keen musician.

169. PRAGUE.

WHITE, HENRY KIRKE. The first line of his poem on 'The Star of Bethlehem' should read: 'Once on the raging seas I rode'.

WILLIAMS, ISAAC, was curate at the Gloucestershire Bisley. Dean Church said of him that 'he had the true poetic gift, though his power of expression was often not equal to what he wanted to say'. See also note on Hymn 292.

WILLIAMS, THOMAS. See in this Supplement note on LLANDINAM under Hymn 65.

WILSON, DAVID FREDERICK RUDDELL, was general editor of *The Church Hymnal* of the Episcopal Church of Ireland, and of *The Irish Chant-book*.

WILSON, JOHN (Edinburgh, 1800–49, Quebec), was early apprenticed to a firm of printers in Edinburgh, and later became proof-reader to Ballantyne, the printer of the *Waverley Novels*. He studied music under John Mather (*vide* William Mather) and Benjamin Gleadhill, and was a member of the choir of Duddingston Church under the ministry of John Thomson, the landscape-painter. He had a very fine tenor voice, and when he became precentor of Roxburgh Place Relief Church his singing and fine taste drew crowds to the church. In 1825 he passed to the precentorship of St. Mary's Parish Church, and edited in the same year *A Selection of Psalm Tunes, Sanctuses, Doxologies, &c.*, for the use of that congregation. Soon afterwards he devoted himself entirely to the study and teaching of music. In 1830 he resigned his post in St. Mary's and took to the stage. His first appearance in opera was in *Guy Mannering*, in Edinburgh. Later, he appeared at Covent Garden and Drury Lane. Finally, he became famous as an exponent of Scottish song, and as such sang before Queen Victoria at Taymouth Castle in 1842. While on tour he died at Quebec. When David Kennedy, another renowned Scots vocalist and erstwhile precentor, visited that city many years afterwards, he restored Wilson's tomb and left a sum of money for its proper preservation.

70. HOWARD (Wilson's *Collection*, 1825).

WILSON, MATTHEW (*c.* 1812–56, Glasgow), in an advertisement in *The Glasgow Herald* for Aug. 28, 1835, described himself as Conductor of the Music in St. Enoch's Church, and as teacher of the piano, singing, and musical composition. One of his pupils has left it on record that he was a good player and teacher, but that it was evident that he had difficulty in making ends meet. Apparently music alone did not suffice to provide a living for him, for he is known to have been for a time a 'traveller' for a tea merchant in the city. He was much in demand as accompanist at free-and-easy concerts in the city. Latterly he seems to have been in deep waters, for in the Glasgow Directory his name does not appear in the lists of teachers of music between 1850 and the year of his death. Another of his tunes appeared under the name 'Union Street' in *The Sacred Harp* of 1840, in which 'Drumclog' is found. He was best known as composer of popular songs, five of which (Nos. 8, 10, 13, 14, 21) are, in *The Lyric Gems of Scotland* (Glasgow, 1856), all to words by William Cameron. Some of these, notably *Morag's Faery Glen*, had great popularity in their day.

49. DRUMCLOG.

WOODWARD, GEORGE. Of this composer's identity nothing has been determined.

114. CHANT IN B♭.

WOODWARD, RICHARD, Mus.Doc. (Dublin, 1744–77, Dublin), son of a vicar choral of Christ Church and St. Patrick's Cathedrals,

Dublin, was a chorister of the former and became organist in 1765; vicar choral in St. Patrick's, 1772. In 1771 he published a folio volume of his church music—one complete service, seven anthems, several chants, and a *Veni Creator Spiritus*. He published also a collection of songs, catches, and canons such as were popular in those days. For the most part his anthems are forgotten, but certain of his chants, notably the double one in D, are still in use. One of his canons, 'Let the words of my mouth', is engraved on his tomb in Christ Church Cathedral.

145. CHANT (D) IN A♭.

61–121. CHANT IN C.   *21*. CHANT (D) IN D.

WRIGHT, Thomas (Stockton-on-Tees, 1763–1829, Wycliffe Keeley, near Barnard Castle), son of Robert Wright, organist in Stockton Church, 1766–97, and grandson of Thomas Wright the elder, who was the first organist of Stockton, *c.* 1758–60; was organist at Sedgefield, nine miles from Stockton, 1785–97, and soon acquired a high reputation as a teacher of piano, violin, and organ, and as an extemporizer on the organ; succeeded his father in Stockton Church, 1797, and continued there till 1817, when he resigned. After a period at Kirkleathen, near Redcar, he returned to Stockton and resumed teaching. He was in great demand as a music-teacher in the county of Durham and the North Riding of Yorkshire, and it was while fulfilling a professional service at Wycliffe Keeley that he was seized with fatal illness and died in the rectory there. He composed *Rusticity*, an operetta; a simple anthem, several songs, and a Concerto for piano and harpsichord, notable as being the first music to contain metronome marks to indicate speed value. He had a remarkable inventive gift, and produced a simple pocket metronome, an organ attachment to a square pianoforte, and other ingenious devices.

132. STOCKTON.

YATTENDON HYMNAL.—Last line. For 248 read 284.

133

PRINTED IN
GREAT BRITAIN
AT THE
UNIVERSITY PRESS
OXFORD
BY
JOHN JOHNSON
PRINTER
TO THE
UNIVERSITY